TypeScript Design Patterns

Boost your development efficiency by learning about design patterns in TypeScript

Vilic Vane

[PACKT] open source
PUBLISHING   community experience distilled

BIRMINGHAM - MUMBAI

TypeScript Design Patterns

First published: August 2016

Production reference: 1240816

Published by Packt Publishing Ltd.
Livery Place
35 Livery Street
Birmingham
B3 2PB, UK.
ISBN 978-1-78528-083-2

www.packtpub.com www.packtpub.com

Credits

Author

Vilic Vane

Copy Editor

Safis Editing

Reviewer

Wander Wang

Project Coordinator

Suzanne Coutinho

Commissioning Editor

Kunal Parikh

Proofreader

Safis Editing

Acquisition Editor

Denim Pinto

Indexer

Rekha Nair

Content Development Editor

Nikhil Borkar

Graphics

Jason Monteiro

Technical Editor

Hussain Kanchwala

Production Coordinator

Aparna Bhagat

About the Author

Vilic Vane is a JavaScript engineer with over 8 years of experience in web development. He started following the TypeScript project since it went public, and he's also a contributor of the project. He is now working at Ruff, a startup company building an IoT platform that runs JavaScript on embedded devices.

I want to thank the editors and reviewers, including Wander Wang, for their efforts that made this book possible. I also want to thank my girlfriend, Emi, for not pissing me off when she came for me from her school 1,400 km away but could only have a takeout with me in my apartment due to my always-about-to-start-writing condition.

About the Reviewer

Wander Wang is working at Egret Technology Co., Ltd. as the chief architect of Egret Engine. He also works as a part-time teacher in the School of Software Engineering at Beijing University of Technology. Wang has 7 years of experience in developing web and mobile games, and he currently focuses on the language research and extension of TypeScript. Egret Engine is a popular HTML5 game engine written in TypeScript. There are more than 80,000 developers worldwide who build their web or mobile games on the top of Egret Engine. Wang is also interested in technologies such as React, React-Native, and Electron, and so on.

www.PacktPub.com

eBooks, discount offers, and more

Did you know that Packt offers eBook versions of every book published, with PDF and ePub files available? You can upgrade to the eBook version at www.PacktPub.com and as a print book customer, you are entitled to a discount on the eBook copy. Get in touch with us at customercare@packtpub.com for more details.

At www.PacktPub.com, you can also read a collection of free technical articles, sign up for a range of free newsletters and receive exclusive discounts and offers on Packt books and eBooks.

https://www2.packtpub.com/books/subscription/packtlib

Do you need instant solutions to your IT questions? PacktLib is Packt's online digital book library. Here, you can search, access, and read Packt's entire library of books.

Why subscribe?

- Fully searchable across every book published by Packt
- Copy and paste, print, and bookmark content
- On demand and accessible via a web browser

Table of Contents

Preface

It wasn't a long time ago that many JavaScript engineers or, most of the time, web frontend engineers, were still focusing on solving detailed technical issues, such as how to lay out specific content cross-browsers and how to send requests cross-domains.

At that time, a good web frontend engineer was usually expected to have notable experience on how detailed features can be implemented with existing APIs. Only a few people cared about how to write application-scale JavaScript because the interaction on a web page was really simple and no one wrote ASP in JavaScript.

However, the situation has changed tremendously. JavaScript has become the only language that runs everywhere, cross-platform and cross-device. In the main battlefield, interactions on the Web become more and more complex, and people are moving business logic from the backend to the frontend. With the growth of the Node.js community, JavaScript is playing a more and more important roles in our life.

I am currently working for an IoT company called Ruff that builds a platform for JavaScript to write applications run on embedded devices. You might have seen a fake book cover in the title of *Writing Device Drivers in JavaScript*, but that is actually a part of what we do.

The boom of JavaScript, however, makes people realize that the language itself might not be powerful enough for applications on a larger scale. While we enjoy the flexibility of the language, we suffer from its lack of static-type information; for instance, consider the following:

- **No static type checking:** We have to rely on debugging or tests to get rid of simple errors that could be eliminated when the code is written.
- **Refactoring is a pain:** Basically, what the IDEs or editors can do about JavaScript code is renaming local variables or exported module functions at best.
- **Understanding code is difficult:** When you grasp a piece of code, you might have to look around and manually search for references just to figure out which properties an object has and what types of property they are. This happens to our own code as well.

Compared to tools such as ESLint and even Flow, which only partially solve the problems, TypeScript does a really good job while it is still sticking to the ECMAScript standard.

TypeScript is indeed an awesome tool for JavaScript. Unfortunately, intelligence is still required to write actually robust, maintainable, and reusable code. But wait, doesn't the intelligence part involve the true value of our work?

We might all have had trouble finding clues to mysterious bugs, or squeezed our head thinking about how we can add new features to the existing code base. Some of us, with experience and intuition built over the years, may directly come up with a design that's not bad. For these people, getting through the common design patterns can help gain knowledge of what people have already catalogued over years in the industry or be better understood when discussing software designs with others. For people who have less experience, learning common design patterns may be a more straightforward approach to creating code that's beautifully designed.

What this book covers

Chapter 1, *Tools and Frameworks*, provides a brief introduction to tools and frameworks that will be used through this book, including installing a TypeScript compiler, preparing an editor, and a basic workflow.

Chapter 2, *The Challenge of Increasing Complexity*, starts with a simple server-client synchronizing implementation; we then expand its features and see how things can gain undesired complexity and how that complexity can be reduced.

Chapter 3, *Creational Design Patterns*, catalogs five common creational design patterns, the Factory Method, Abstract Factory, Builder, Prototype, and Singleton patterns.

Chapter 4, *Structural Design Patterns*, catalogs seven common structural design patterns, the Composite, Decorator, Adapter, Bridge, Façade, Flyweight, and Proxy patterns.

Chapter 5, *Behavioral Design Patterns*, catalogs five common behavioral design patterns, the Chain of Responsibility, Command, Memento, Iterator, and Mediator patterns.

Chapter 6, *Behavioral Design Patterns: Continuous*, catalogs another four common behavioral design patterns, the Strategy, State, Template Method, Observer, and Visitor patterns.

Chapter 7, *Patterns and Architectures in JavaScript and TypeScript*, takes a look at the patterns and architectures that closely relate to the language (JavaScript or TypeScript) and its application, including asynchronous programming, module organization, error handling, permission abstraction, and so on.

Chapter 8, *SOLID Principles*, explains the well-known SOLID principles and how they can benefit a project and keep it healthy over time.

Chapter 9, *The Road to Enterprise Application*, guides readers to build the complete workflow of an application that is ready to scale, including testing and continuous integration.

What you need for this book

It is possible to read through this entire book without installing anything. But it is recommended that you have a handy editor and TypeScript compiler installed to get your hands dirty. Please refer to Chapter 1, *Tools and Frameworks,* for the detailed preparation of tools, including Node.js, a TypeScript compiler, declaration manager, and a nice editor or IDE.

Though this book does not require the reader to have a knowledge of design patterns, it's not a book that teaches basic TypeScript syntax. If you are not yet familiar with TypeScript, please walk through the TypeScript Handbook before reading Chapter 2, *The Challenge of Increasing Complexity.*

Who this book is for

If you are a TypeScript developer, this book is for you. No knowledge of design patterns is required to read this book.

Conventions

In this book, you will find a number of text styles that distinguish between different kinds of information. Here are some examples of these styles and an explanation of their meaning.

Code words in text, database table names, folder names, filenames, file extensions, pathnames, dummy URLs, user input, and Twitter handles are shown as follows: "Save the following code to file test.ts."

A block of code is set as follows:

```
require('chai').should();
```

Any command-line input or output is written as follows:

```
$ tsc test.ts
```

New terms and **important words** are shown in bold. Words that you see on the screen, for example, in menus or dialog boxes, appear in the text like this: "Without the necessary declaration files, the compiler would complain **Cannot find module express**."

Warnings or important notes appear in a box like this.

 Tips and tricks appear like this.

Reader feedback

Feedback from our readers is always welcome. Let us know what you think about this book-what you liked or disliked. Reader feedback is important for us as it helps us develop titles that you will really get the most out of. To send us general feedback, simply e-mail feedback@packtpub.com, and mention the book's title in the subject of your message. If there is a topic that you have expertise in and you are interested in either writing or contributing to a book, see our author guide at www.packtpub.com/authors.

Customer support

Now that you are the proud owner of a Packt book, we have a number of things to help you to get the most from your purchase.

Downloading the example code

You can download the example code files for this book from your account at http://www.packtpub.com. If you purchased this book elsewhere, you can visit http://www.packtpub.com/support and register to have the files e-mailed directly to you.

You can download the code files by following these steps:

1. Log in or register to our website using your e-mail address and password.
2. Hover the mouse pointer on the **SUPPORT** tab at the top.
3. Click on **Code Downloads & Errata**.
4. Enter the name of the book in the **Search** box.
5. Select the book for which you're looking to download the code files.
6. Choose from the drop-down menu where you purchased this book from.
7. Click on **Code Download**.

Once the file is downloaded, please make sure that you unzip or extract the folder using the latest version of:

- WinRAR / 7-Zip for Windows
- Zipeg / iZip / UnRarX for Mac
- 7-Zip / PeaZip for Linux

The code bundle for the book is also hosted on GitHub at `https://github.com/PacktPublishing/TypeScript-Design-Patterns/`. We also have other code bundles from our rich catalog of books and videos available at `https://github.com/PacktPublishing/`. Check them out!

Errata

Although we have taken every care to ensure the accuracy of our content, mistakes do happen. If you find a mistake in one of our books-maybe a mistake in the text or the code-we would be grateful if you could report this to us. By doing so, you can save other readers from frustration and help us improve subsequent versions of this book. If you find any errata, please report them by visiting `http://www.packtpub.com/submit-errata`, selecting your book, clicking on the **Errata Submission Form** link, and entering the details of your errata. Once your errata are verified, your submission will be accepted and the errata will be uploaded to our website or added to any list of existing errata under the Errata section of that title.

To view the previously submitted errata, go to `https://www.packtpub.com/books/content/support` and enter the name of the book in the search field. The required information will appear under the **Errata** section.

Piracy

Piracy of copyrighted material on the Internet is an ongoing problem across all media. At Packt, we take the protection of our copyright and licenses very seriously. If you come across any illegal copies of our works in any form on the Internet, please provide us with the location address or website name immediately so that we can pursue a remedy.

Please contact us at `copyright@packtpub.com` with a link to the suspected pirated material.

We appreciate your help in protecting our authors and our ability to bring you valuable content.

Questions

If you have a problem with any aspect of this book, you can contact us at `questions@packtpub.com`, and we will do our best to address the problem.

1
Tools and Frameworks

We could always use the help of real code to explain the design patterns we'll be discussing. In this chapter, we'll have a brief introduction to the tools and frameworks that you might need if you want to have some practice with complete working implementations of the contents of this book.

In this chapter, we'll cover the following topics:

- Installing Node.js and TypeScript compiler
- Popular editors or IDEs for TypeScript
- Configuring a TypeScript project
- A basic workflow that you might need to play with your own implementations of the design patterns in this book

Installing the prerequisites

The contents of this chapter are expected to work on all major and up-to-date desktop operating systems, including Windows, OS X, and Linux.

As Node.js is widely used as a runtime for server applications as well as frontend build tools, we are going to make it the main playground of code in this book.

TypeScript compiler, on the other hand, is the tool that compiles TypeScript source files into plain JavaScript. It's available on multiple platforms and runtimes, and in this book we'll be using the Node.js version.

Installing Node.js

Installing Node.js should be easy enough. But there's something we could do to minimize incompatibility over time and across different environments:

- **Version**: We'll be using Node.js 6 with npm 3 built-in in this book. (The major version of Node.js may increase rapidly over time, but we can expect minimum breaking changes directly related to our contents. Feel free to try a newer version if it's available.)
- **Path**: If you are installing Node.js without a package manager, make sure the environment variable PATH is properly configured.

Open a console (a command prompt or terminal, depending on your operating system) and make sure Node.js as well as the built-in package manager npm is working:

```
$ node -v
6.x.x
$ npm -v
3.x.x
```

Installing TypeScript compiler

TypeScript compiler for Node.js is published as an npm package with command line interface. To install the compiler, we can simply use the npm install command:

```
$ npm install typescript -g
```

Option -g means a global installation, so that tsc will be available as a command. Now let's make sure the compiler works:

```
$ tsc -v
Version 2.x.x
```

 You may get a rough list of the options your TypeScript compiler provides with switch -h. Taking a look into these options may help you discover some useful features.

Before choosing an editor, let's print out the legendary phrase:

1. Save the following code to file test.ts:

```
function hello(name: string): void {
  console.log(`hello, ${name}!`);
}

hello('world');
```

2. Change the working directory of your console to the folder containing the created file, and compile it with tsc:

```
$ tsc test.ts
```

3. With luck, you should have the compiled JavaScript file as test.js. Execute it with Node.js to get the ceremony done:

```
$ node test.js
hello, world!
```

Here we go, on the road to retire your CTO.

Choosing a handy editor

A compiler without a good editor won't be enough (if you are not a believer of Notepad). Thanks to the efforts made by the TypeScript community, there are plenty of great editors and IDEs ready for TypeScript development.

However, the choice of an editor could be much about personal preferences. In this section, we'll talk about the installation and configuration of Visual Studio Code and Sublime Text. But other popular editors or IDEs for TypeScript will also be listed with brief introductions.

Visual Studio Code

Visual Studio Code is a free lightweight editor written in TypeScript. And it's an open source and cross-platform editor that already has TypeScript support built-in.

You can download Visual Studio Code from https://code.visualstudio.com/ and the installation will probably take no more than 1 minute.

The following screenshot shows the debugging interface of Visual Studio Code with a TypeScript source file:

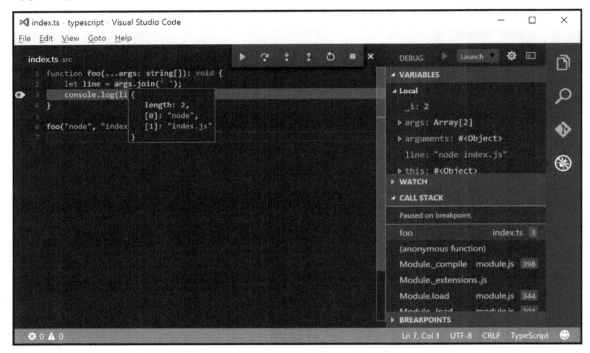

Configuring Visual Studio Code

As Code already has TypeScript support built-in, extra configurations are actually not required. But if the version of TypeScript compiler you use to compile the source code differs from what Code has built-in, it could result in unconformity between editing and compiling.

To stay away from the undesired issues this would bring, we need to configure TypeScript SDK used by Visual Studio Code manually:

1. Press *F1*, type `Open User Settings`, and enter. Visual Studio Code will open the settings JSON file by the side of a read-only JSON file containing all the default settings.
2. Add the field `typescript.tsdk` with the path of the `lib` folder under the TypeScript package we previously installed:

   1. Execute the command `npm root -g` in your console to get the root of global Node.js modules.

   2. Append the root path with `/typescript/lib` as the SDK path.

 You can also have a TypeScript package installed locally with the project, and use the local TypeScript `lib` path for Visual Studio Code. (You will need to use the locally installed version for compiling as well.)

Opening a folder as a workspace

Visual Studio Code is a file- and folder-based editor, which means you can open a file or a folder and start work.

But you still need to properly configure the project to take the best advantage of Code. For TypeScript, the project file is `tsconfig.json`, which contains the description of source files and compiler options. Know little about `tsconfig.json`? Don't worry, we'll come to that later.

Here are some features of Visual Studio Code you might be interested in:

- **Tasks**: Basic task integration. You can build your project without leaving the editor.
- **Debugging**: Node.js debugging with source map support, which means you can debug Node.js applications written in TypeScript.
- **Git**: Basic Git integration. This makes comparing and committing changes easier.

Configuring a minimum build task

The default key binding for a build task is *Ctrl + Shift + B* or *cmd + Shift + B* on OS X. By pressing these keys, you will get a prompt notifying you that no task runner has been configured. Click **Configure Task Runner** and then select a TypeScript build task template (either with or without the watch mode enabled). A `tasks.json` file under the `.vscode` folder will be created automatically with content similar to the following:

```
{
    "version": "0.1.0",
    "command": "tsc",
    "isShellCommand": true,
    "args": ["-w", "-p", "."],
    "showOutput": "silent",
    "isWatching": true,
    "problemMatcher": "$tsc-watch"
}
```

Now create a `test.ts` file with some hello-world code and run the build task again. You can either press the shortcut we mentioned before or press Ctrl/Cmd + P, type `task tsc`, and enter.

If you were doing things correctly, you should be seeing the output `test.js` by the side of `test.ts`.

There are some useful configurations for tasking that can't be covered. You may find more information on the website of Visual Studio Code: `https://code.visualstudio.com/`.

From my perspective, Visual Studio Code delivers the best TypeScript development experience in the class of code editors. But if you are not a fan of it, TypeScript is also available with official support for Sublime Text.

Sublime Text with TypeScript plugin

Sublime Text is another popular lightweight editor around the field with amazing performance.

The following image shows how TypeScript IntelliSense works in Sublime Text:

The TypeScript team has officially built a plugin for Sublime Text (version 3 preferred), and you can find a detailed introduction, including useful shortcuts, in their GitHub repository here: `https://github.com/Microsoft/TypeScript-Sublime-Plugin`.

 There are still some issues with the TypeScript plugin for Sublime Text. It would be nice to know about them before you start writing TypeScript with Sublime Text.

Installing Package Control

Package Control is de facto package manager for Sublime Text, with which we'll install the TypeScript plugin.

If you don't have Package Control installed, perform the following steps:

1. Click **Preferences** > **Browse Packages…**, it opens the Sublime Text packages folder.
2. Browse up to the parent folder and then into the **Install Packages** folder, and download the file below into this folder: `https://packagecontrol.io/Package%2Control.sublime-package`
3. Restart Sublime Text and you should now have a working package manager.

Now we are only one step away from IntelliSense and refactoring with Sublime Text.

Installing the TypeScript plugin

With the help of Package Control, it's easy to install a plugin:

1. Open the Sublime Text editor; press Ctrl + Shift + P for Windows and Linux or Cmd + Shift + P for OS X.
2. Type `Install Package` in the command palette, select **Package Control: Install Package** and wait for it to load the plugin repositories.
3. Type `TypeScript` and select to install the official plugin.

Now we have TypeScript ready for Sublime Text, cheers!

Like Visual Studio Code, unmatched TypeScript versions between the plugin and compiler could lead to problems. To fix this, you can add the field `"typescript_tsdk"` with a path to the TypeScript `lib` in the **Settings – User** file.

Other editor or IDE options

Visual Studio Code and Sublime Text are recommended due to their ease of use and popularity respectively. But there are many great tools from the editor class to full-featured IDE.

Though we're not going through the setup and configuration of those tools, you might want to try them out yourself, especially if you are already working with some of them.

However, the configuration for different editors and IDEs (especially IDEs) could differ. It is recommended to use Visual Studio Code or Sublime Text for going through the workflow and examples in this book.

Atom with the TypeScript plugin

Atom is a cross-platform editor created by GitHub. It has a notable community with plenty of useful plugins, including `atom-typescript`. `atom-typescript` is the result of the hard work of Basarat Ali Syed, and it's used by my team before Visual Studio Code. It has many handy features that Visual Studio Code does not have yet, such as module path suggestion, compile on save, and so on.

Like Visual Studio Code, Atom is also an editor based on web technologies. Actually, the shell used by Visual Studio Code is exactly what's used by Atom: Electron, another popular project by GitHub, for building cross-platform desktop applications.

Atom is proud of being hackable, which means you can customize your own Atom editor pretty much as you want.

Then you may be wondering why we turned to Visual Studio Code. The main reason is that Visual Studio Code is being backed by the same company that develops TypeScript, and another reason might be the performance issue with Atom.

But anyway, Atom could be a great choice for a start.

Visual Studio

Visual Studio is one of the best IDEs in the market. And yet it has, of course, official TypeScript support.

Since Visual Studio 2013, a community version is provided for free to individual developers, small companies, and open source projects.

If you are looking for a powerful IDE of TypeScript on Windows, Visual Studio could be a wonderful choice. Though Visual Studio has built-in TypeScript support, do make sure it's up-to-date. And, usually, you might want to install the newest TypeScript tools for Visual Studio.

WebStorm

WebStorm is one of the most popular IDEs for JavaScript developers, and it has had an early adoption to TypeScript as well.

A downside of using WebStorm for TypeScript is that it is always one step slower catching up to the latest version compared to other major editors. Unlike editors that directly use the language service provided by the TypeScript project, WebStorm seems to have its own infrastructure for IntelliSense and refactoring. But, in return, it makes TypeScript support in WebStorm more customizable and consistent with other features it provides.

If you decide to use WebStorm as your TypeScript IDE, please make sure the version of supported TypeScript matches what you expect (usually the latest version).

Getting your hands on the workflow

After setting up your editor, we are ready to move to a workflow that you might use to practice throughout this book. It can also be used as the workflow for small TypeScript projects in your daily work.

In this workflow, we'll walk through these topics:

- What is a `tsconfig.json` file, and how can you configure a TypeScript project with it?
- TypeScript declaration files and the `typings` command-line tool
- How to write tests running under Mocha, and how to get coverage information using Istanbul
- How to test in browsers using Karma

Configuring a TypeScript project

The configurations of a TypeScript project can differ for a variety of reasons. But the goals remain clear: we need the editor as well as the compiler to recognize a project and its source files correctly. And `tsconfig.json` will do the job.

Introduction to tsconfig.json

A TypeScript project does not have to contain a tsconfig.json file. However, most editors rely on this file to recognize a TypeScript project with specified configurations and to provide related features.

A tsconfig.json file accepts three fields: compilerOptions, files, and exclude. For example, a simple tsconfig.json file could be like the following:

```
{
  "compilerOptions": {
    "target": "es5",
    "module": "commonjs",
    "rootDir": "src",
    "outDir": "out"
  },
  "exclude": [
    "out",
    "node_modules"
  ]
}
```

Or, if you prefer to manage the source files manually, it could be like this:

```
{
  "compilerOptions": {
    "target": "es5",
    "module": "commonjs",
    "rootDir": "src",
    "outDir": "out"
  },
  "files": [
    "src/foo.ts",
    "src/bar.ts"
  ]
}
```

Previously, when we used tsc, we needed to specify the source files explicitly. Now, with tsconfig.json, we can directly run tsc without arguments (or with -w/--watch if you want incremental compilation) in a folder that contains tsconfig.json.

Compiler options

As TypeScript is still evolving, its compiler options keep changing, with new features and updates. An invalid option may break the compilation or editor features for TypeScript. When reading these options, keep in mind that some of them might have been changed.

The following options are useful ones out of the list.

target

`target` specifies the expected version of JavaScript outputs. It could be `es5` (ECMAScript 5), `es6` (ECMAScript 6/2015), and so on.

Features (especially ECMAScript polyfills) that are available in different compilation targets vary. For example, before TypeScript 2.1, features such as `async`/`await` were available only when targeting ES6.

The good news is that Node.js 6 with the latest V8 engine has supported most ES6 features. And the latest browsers have also great ES6 support. So if you are developing a Node.js application or a browser application that's not required for backward compatibilities, you can have your configuration target ES6.

module

Before ES6, JavaScript had no standard module system. Varieties of module loaders are developed for different scenarios, such as `commonjs`, `amd`, `umd`, `system`, and so on.

If you are developing a Node.js application or an npm package, `commonjs` could be the value of this option. Actually, with the help of modern packaging tools such as webpack and browserify, commonjs could also be a nice choice for browser projects as well.

declaration

Enable this option to generate `.d.ts` declaration files along with JavaScript outputs. Declaration files could be useful as the type information source of a distributed library/framework; it could also be helpful for splitting a larger project to improve compiling performance and division cooperation.

sourceMap

By enabling this option, TypeScript compiler will emit source maps along with compiled JavaScript.

jsx

TypeScript provides built-in support for React JSX (`.tsx`) files. By specifying this option with value `react`, TypeScript compiler will compile `.tsx` files to plain JavaScript files. Or with value `preserve`, it will output `.jsx` files so you can post-process these files with other JSX compilers.

noEmitOnError

By default, TypeScript will emit outputs no matter whether type errors are found or not. If this is not what you want, you may set this option to `true`.

noEmitHelpers

When compiling a newer ECMAScript feature to a lower target version of JavaScript, TypeScript compiler will sometimes generate helper functions such as `__extends` (ES6 to lower versions), and `__awaiter` (ES7 to lower versions).

Due to certain reasons, you may want to write your own helper functions, and prevent TypeScript compiler from emitting these helpers.

noImplicitAny

As TypeScript is a superset of JavaScript, it allows variables and parameters to have no type notation. However, it could help to make sure everything is typed.

By enabling this option, TypeScript compiler will give errors if the type of a variable/parameter is not specified and cannot be inferred by its context.

experimentalDecorators*

As decorators, at the time of writing this book, has not yet reached a stable stage of the new ECMAScript standard, you need to enable this option to use decorators.

emitDecoratorMetadata*

Runtime type information could sometimes be useful, but TypeScript does not yet support reflection (maybe it never will). Luckily, we get decorator metadata that will help under certain scenarios.

By enabling this option, TypeScript will emit decorators along with a `Reflect.metadata()` decorator which contains the type information of the decorated target.

outDir

Usually, we do not want compiled files to be in the same folder of source code. By specifying `outDir`, you can tell the compiler where you would want the compiled JavaScript files to be.

outFile

For small browser projects, we might want to have all the outputs concatenated as a single file. By enabling this option, we can achieve that without extra build tools.

rootDir

The `rootDir` option is to specify the root of the source code. If omitted, the compiler would use the longest common path of source files. This might take seconds to understand.

For example, if we have two source files, `src/foo.ts` and `src/bar.ts`, and a `tsconfig.json` file in the same directory of the `src` folder, the TypeScript compiler will use `src` as the `rootDir`, so when emitting files to the `outDir` (let's say out), they will be `out/foo.js` and `out/bar.js`.

However, if we add another source file `test/test.ts` and compile again, we'll get those outputs located in `out/src/foo.js`, `out/src/bar.js`, and `out/test/test.js` respectively. When calculating the longest common path, declaration files are not involved as they have no output.

Usually, we don't need to specify `rootDir`, but it would be safer to have it configured.

preserveConstEnums

Enum is a useful tool provided by TypeScript. When compiled, it's in the form of an `Enum.member` expression. Constant enum, on the other hand, emits number literals directly, which means the `Enum` object is no longer necessary.

And thus TypeScript, by default, will remove the definitions of constant enums in the compiled JavaScript files.

By enabling this option, you can force the compiler to keep these definitions anyway.

strictNullChecks

TypeScript 2.1 makes it possible to explicitly declare a type with `undefined` or `null` as its subtype. And the compiler can now perform more thorough type checking for empty values if this option is enabled.

stripInternal*

When emitting declaration files, there could be something you'll need to use internally but without a better way to specify the accessibility. By commenting this code with `/** @internal */` (JSDoc annotation), TypeScript compiler then won't emit them to declaration files.

isolatedModules

By enabling this option, the compiler will unconditionally emit imports for unresolved files.

 Options suffixed with * are experimental and might have already been removed when you are reading this book. For a more complete and up-to-date compiler options list, please check out `http://www.typescriptlang.org/docs/handbook/compiler-options.html`.

Adding source map support

Source maps can help a lot while debugging, no matter for a debugger or for error stack traces from a log.

To have source map support, we need to enable the `sourceMap` compiler option in `tsconfig.json`. Extra configurations might be necessary to make your debugger work with source maps.

For error stack traces, we can use the help of the `source-map-support` package:

```
$ npm install source-map-support --save
```

To put it into effect, you can import this package with its `register` submodule in your entry file:

```
import 'source-map-support/register';
```

Downloading declarations using typings

JavaScript has a large and booming ecosystem. As the bridge connecting TypeScript and other JavaScript libraries and frameworks, declaration files are playing a very important role.

With the help of declaration files, TypeScript developer can use existing JavaScript libraries with nearly the same experience as libraries written in TypeScript.

Thanks to the efforts of the TypeScript community, almost every popular JavaScript library or framework got its declaration files on a project called *DefinitelyTyped*. And there has already been a tool called `tsd` for declaration file management. But soon, people realized the limitation of a single huge repository for everything, as well as the issues `tsd` cannot solve nicely. Then `typings` is gently becoming the new tool for TypeScript declaration file management.

Installing typings

`typings` is just another Node.js package with a command-line interface like TypeScript compiler. To install `typings`, simply execute the following:

```
$ npm install typings -g
```

To make sure it has been installed correctly, you can now try the `typings` command with argument `--version`:

```
$ typings --version
1.x.x
```

Downloading declaration files

Create a basic Node.js project with a proper `tsconfig.json` (module option set as `commonjs`), and a `test.ts` file:

```
import * as express from 'express';
```

Without the necessary declaration files, the compiler would complain with **Cannot find module express**. And, actually, you can't even use Node.js APIs such as `process.exit()` or require Node.js modules, because TypeScript itself just does not know what Node.js is.

To begin with, we'll need to install declaration files of Node.js and Express:

```
$ typings install env~node --global
$ typings install express
```

If everything goes fine, `typings` should've downloaded several declaration files and saved them to folder `typings`, including `node.d.ts`, `express.d.ts`, and so on. And I guess you've already noticed the dependency relationship existing on declaration files.

 If this is not working for you and `typings` complains with **Unable to find "express" ("npm") in the registry** then you might need to do it the hard way – to manually install Express declaration files and their dependencies using the following command:
$ typings install dt~<package-name> –global
The reason for that is the community might still be moving from `DefinitelyTyped` to the `typings` registry. The prefix `dt~` tells `typings` to download declaration files from `DefintelyTyped`, and `--global` option tells `typings` to save these declaration files as ambient modules (namely declarations with module name specified).

`typings` has several registries, and the default one is called npm (please understand this npm registry is not the `npm` package registry). So, if no registry is specified with `<source>~` prefix or `--source` option, it will try to find declaration files from its npm registry. This means that `typings install express` is equivalent to `typings install npm~express` or `typings install express --source npm`.

While declaration files for npm packages are usually available on the npm registry, declaration files for the environment are usually available on the env. registry. As those declarations are usually global, a `--global` option is required for them to install correctly.

Option "save"

`typings` actually provides a `--save` option for saving the typing names and file sources to `typings.json`. However, in my opinion, this option is not practically useful.

It's great to have the most popular JavaScript libraries and frameworks typed, but these declaration files, especially declarations not frequently used, can be inaccurate, which means there's a fair chance that you will need to edit these files yourself.

It would be nice to contribute declarations, but it would also be more flexible to have `typings` m managed by source control as part of the project code.

Testing with Mocha and Istanbul

Testing could be an important part of a project, which ensures feature consistency and discovers bugs earlier. It is common that a change made for one feature could break another working part of the project. A robust design could minimize the chance but we still need tests to make sure.

It could lead to an endless discussion about how tests should be written and there are interesting code design techniques such as **test-driven development** (**TDD**); though there has been a lot of debates around it, it still worth knowing and may inspire you in certain ways.

Mocha and Chai

Mocha has been one of the most popular test frameworks for JavaScript, while Chai is a good choice as an assertion library. To make life easier, you may write tests for your own implementations of contents through this book using Mocha and Chai.

To install Mocha, simply run the following command, and it will add `mocha` as a global command-line tool just like `tsc` and `typings`:

```
$ npm install mocha -g
```

Chai, on the other hand, is used as a module of a project, and should be installed under the project folder as a development dependency:

```
$ npm install chai --save-dev
```

Chai supports `should` style assertion. By invoking `chai.should()`, it adds the `should` property to the prototype of `Object`, which means you can then write assertions such as the following:

```
'foo'.should.not.equal('bar');
'typescript'.should.have.length(10);
```

Writing tests in JavaScript

By executing the command `mocha`, it will automatically run tests inside the `test` folder. Before we start to write tests in TypeScript, let's try it out in plain JavaScript and make sure it's working.

Create a file `test/starter.js` and save it with the following code:

```
require('chai').should();

describe('some feature', () => {
  it('should pass', () => {
    'foo'.should.not.equal('bar');
  });

  it('should error', () => {
    (() => {
      throw new Error();
    }).should.throw();
  });
});
```

Run `mocha` under the project folder and you should see all tests passing.

Writing tests in TypeScript

Tests written in TypeScript have to be compiled before being run; where to put those files could be a tricky question to answer.

Some people might want to separate tests with their own `tsconfig.json`:

```
src/tsconfig.json
test/tsconfig.json
```

They may also want to put output files somewhere reasonable:

```
out/app/
out/test/
```

However, this will increase the cost of build process management for small projects. So, if you do not mind having `src` in the paths of your compiled files, you can have only one `tsconfig.json` to get the job done:

```
src/
test/
tsconfig.json
```

The destinations will be as follows:

```
out/src/
out/test/
```

Another option I personally prefer is to have tests inside of `src/test`, and use the `test` folder under the project root for Mocha configurations:

```
src/
src/test/
tsconfig.json
```

The destinations will be as follows:

```
out/
out/test/
```

But, either way, we'll need to configure Mocha properly to do the following:

- Run tests under the `out/test` directory
- Configure the assertion library and other tools before starting to run tests

To achieve these, we can take advantage of the `mocha.opts` file instead of specifying command-line arguments every time. Mocha will combine lines in the `mocha.opts` file with other command-line arguments given while being loaded.

Create `test/mocha.opts` with the following lines:

```
--require ./test/mocha.js
out/test/
```

As you might have guessed, the first line is to tell Mocha to require `./test/mocha.js` before starting to run actual tests. And the second line tells Mocha where these tests are located.

And, of course, we'll need to create `test/mocha.js` correspondingly:

```
require('chai').should();
```

Almost ready to write tests in TypeScript! But TypeScript compiler does not know how would function `describe` or `it` be like, so we need to download declaration files for Mocha:

```
$ typings install env~mocha --global
```

Now we can migrate the `test/starter.js` file to `src/test/starter.ts` with nearly no change, but removing the first line that enables the `should` style assertion of Chai, as we have already put it into `test/mocha.js`.

Compile and run; buy me a cup of coffee if it works. But it probably won't. We've talked about how TypeScript compiler determines the root of source files when explaining the `rootDir` compiler option. As we don't have any TypeScript files under the `src` folder (not including its subfolders), TypeScript compiler uses `src/test` as the `rootDir`. Thus the compiled test files are now under the `out` folder instead of the expected `out/test`.

To fix this, either explicitly specify `rootDir`, or just add the first non-test TypeScript file to the `src` folder.

Getting coverage information with Istanbul

Coverage could be important for measuring the quality of tests. However, it might take much effort to reach a number close to 100%, which could be a burden for developers. To balance efforts on tests and code that bring direct value to the product, there would go another debate.

Install Istanbul via `npm` just as with the other tools:

```
$ npm install istanbul -g
```

The subcommand for Istanbul to generate code coverage information is `istanbul cover`. It should be followed by a JavaScript file, but we need to make it work with Mocha, which is a command-line tool. Luckily, the entry of the Mocha command is, of course, a JavaScript file.

To make them work together, we'll need to install a local (instead of global) version of Mocha for the project:

```
$ npm install mocha --save-dev
```

After installation, we'll get the file `_mocha` under `node_modules/mocha/bin`, which is the JavaScript entry we were looking for. So now we can make Istanbul work:

```
$ istanbul cover node_modules/mocha/bin/_mocha
```

Then you should've got a folder named `coverage`, and within it the coverage report.

Reviewing the coverage report is important; it can help you decide whether you need to add tests for specific features and code branches.

Testing in real browsers with Karma

We've talked about testing with Mocha and Istanbul for Node.js applications. It is an important topic for testing code that runs in a browser as well.

Karma is a test runner for JavaScript that makes testing in real browsers on real devices much easier. It officially supports the Mocha, Jasmine, and JUnit testing frameworks, but it's also possible for Karma to work with any framework via a simple adapter.

Creating a browser project

A TypeScript application that runs in browsers can be quite different from a Node.js one. But if you know what the project should look like after the build, you should already have clues on how to configure that project.

To avoid introducing too many concepts and technologies not directly related, I will keep things as simple as possible:

- We're not going to use module loaders such as Require.js
- We're not going to touch the code packaging process

This means we'll go with separated output files that need to be put into an HTML file with a `script` tag manually. Here's the `tsconfig.json` we'll be playing with; notice that we no longer have the `module` option, set:

```
{
  "compilerOptions": {
    "target": "es5",
    "rootDir": "src",
    "outDir": "out"
  },
  "exclude": [
    "out",
```

```
     "node_modules"
   ]
}
```

Then let's create `package.json` and install packages `mocha` and `chai` with their declarations:

```
$ npm init
$ npm install mocha chai --save-dev
$ typings install env~mocha --global
$ typings install chai
```

And to begin with, let's fill this project with some source code and tests.

Create `src/index.ts` with the following code:

```
function getLength(str: string): number {
  return str.length;
}
```

And create `src/test/test.ts` with some tests:

```
describe('get length', () => {
  it('"abc" should have length 3', () => {
    getLength('abc').should.equal(3);
  });

  it('"" should have length 0', () => {
    getLength('').should.equal(0);
  });
});
```

Again, in order to make the `should` style assertion work, we'll need to call `chai.should()` before tests start. To do so, create file `test/mocha.js` just like we did in the Node.js project, though the code line slightly differs, as we no longer use modules:

```
chai.should();
```

Now compile these files with `tsc`, and we've got our project ready.

Installing Karma

Karma itself runs on Node.js, and is available as an npm package just like other Node.js tools we've been using. To install Karma, simply execute the `npm install` command in the project directory:

```
$ npm install karma --save-dev
```

And, in our case, we are going to have Karma working with Mocha, Chai, and the browser Chrome, so we'll need to install related plugins:

```
$ npm install karma-mocha karma-chai karma-chrome-launcher --save-dev
```

Before we configure Karma, it is recommended to have `karma-cli` installed globally so that we can execute the `karma` command from the console directly:

```
$ npm install karma-cli -g
```

Configuring and starting Karma

The configurations are to tell Karma about the testing frameworks and browsers you are going to use, as well as other related information such as source files and tests to run.

To create a Karma configuration file, execute `karma init` and answer its questions:

- **Testing framework**: Mocha
- **Require.js**: no
- **Browsers**: Chrome (add more if you like; be sure to install the corresponding launchers)
- **Source and test files**:
    - `test/mocha.js` (the file enables `should` style assertion)
    - `out/*.js` (source files)
    - `out/test/*.js` (test files)
- **Files to exclude**: empty
- **Watch for changes**: yes

Now you should see a `karma.conf.js` file under the project directory; open it with your editor and add `'chai'` to the list of option frameworks.

Almost there! Execute the command `karma start` and, if everything goes fine, you should have specified browsers opened with the testing results being logged in the console in seconds.

Integrating commands with npm

The npm provides a simple but useful way to define custom scripts that can be run with the `npm run` command. And it has another advantage – when `npm run` a custom script, it adds `node_modules/.bin` to the `PATH`. This makes it easier to manage project-related command-line tools.

For example, we've talked about Mocha and Istanbul. The prerequisite for having them as commands is to have them installed globally, which requires extra steps other than `npm install`. Now we can simply save them as development dependencies, and add custom scripts in `package.json`:

```
"scripts": {
  "test": "mocha",
  "cover": "istanbul cover node_modules/mocha/bin/_mocha"
},
"devDependencies": {
  "mocha": "latest",
  "istanbul": "latest"
}
```

Now you can run `test` with `npm run test` (or simply `npm test`), and run `cover` with `npm run cover` without installing these packages globally.

Why not other fancy build tools?

You might be wondering: why don't we use a build system such as Gulp to set up our workflow? Actually, when I started to write this chapter, I did list Gulp as the tool we were going to use. Later, I realized it does not make much sense to use Gulp to build the implementations in most of the chapters in this book.

There is a message I want to deliver: *balance*.

Once, I had a discussion on *balance versus principles* with my boss. The disagreement was clear: he insisted on controllable principles over subjective balance, while I prefer contextual balance over fixed principles.

Actually, I agree with him, from the point of view of a team leader. A team is usually built up with developers at different levels; principles make it easier for a team to build high-quality products, while not everyone is able to find the right balance point.

However, when the role turns from a productive team member to a learner, it is important to learn and to feel the right balance point. And that's called experience.

Summary

The goal of this chapter was to introduce a basic workflow that could be used by the reader to implement the design patterns we'll be discussing.

We talked about the installation of TypeScript compiler that runs on Node.js, and had brief introductions to popular TypeScript editors and IDEs. Later, we spent quite a lot of pages walking through the tools and frameworks that could be used if the reader wants to have some practice with implementations of the patterns in this book.

With the help of these tools and frameworks, we've built a minimum workflow that includes creating, building, and testing a project. And talking about workflows, you must have noticed that they slightly differ among applications for different runtimes.

In the next chapter, we'll talk about what may go wrong and mess up the entire project when its complexity keeps growing. And we'll try to come up with specific patterns that can solve the problems this very project faces.

2
The Challenge of Increasing Complexity

The essence of a program is the combination of possible branches and automated selections based on certain conditions. When we write a program, we define what's going on in a branch, and under what condition this branch will be executed.

The number of branches usually grows quickly during the evolution of a project, as well as the number of conditions that determine whether a branch will be executed or not.

This is dangerous for human beings, who have limited brain capacities.

In this chapter, we are going to implement a data synchronizing service. Starting by implementing some very basic features, we'll keep adding stuff and see how things go.

The following topics will be covered:

- Designing a multi-device synchronizing strategy
- Useful JavaScript and TypeScript techniques and hints that are related, including objects as maps and the string literal type
- How the Strategy Pattern helps in a project

Implementing the basics

Before we start to write actual code, we need to define what this synchronizing strategy will be like. To keep the implementation from unnecessary distractions, the client will communicate with the server directly through function calls instead of using HTTP requests or Sockets. Also, we'll use **in-memory storage**, namely variables, to store data on both client and server sides.

Because we are not separating the client and server into two actual applications, and we are not actually using backend technologies, it does not require much Node.js experience to follow this chapter.

However, please keep in mind that even though we are omitting network and database requests, we hope the core logic of the final implementation could be applied to a real environment without being modified too much. So, when it comes to performance concerns, we still need to assume limited network resources, especially for data passing through the server and client, although the implementation is going to be synchronous instead of asynchronous. This is not supposed to happen in practice, but involving asynchronous operations will introduce much more code, as well as many more situations that need to be taken into consideration. But we will have some useful patterns on asynchronous programming in the coming chapters, and it would definitely help if you try to implement an asynchronous version of the synchronizing logic in this chapter.

A client, if without modifying what's been synchronized, stores a copy of all the data available on the server, and what we need to do is to provide a set of APIs that enable the client to keep its copy of data synchronized.

So, it is really simple at the beginning: comparing the last-modified timestamp. If the timestamp on the client is older than what's on the server, then update the copy of data along with new timestamp.

Creating the code base

Firstly, let's create `server.ts` and `client.ts` files containing the `Server` class and `Client` class respectively:

```
export class Server {
    // ...
}

export class Client {
    // ...
```

```
}
```

I prefer to create an `index.ts` file as the package entry, which handles what to export internally. In this case, let's export everything:

```
export * from './server';
export * from './client';
```

To import the `Server` and `Client` classes from a test file (assuming `src/test/test.ts`), we can use the following codeto s:

```
import { Server, Client } from '../';
```

Defining the initial structure of the data to be synchronized

Since we need to compare the timestamps from the client and server, we need to have a `timestamp` property on the data structure. I would like to have the data to synchronize as a string, so let's add a `DataStore` interface with a `timestamp` property to the `server.ts` file:

```
export interface DataStore {
  timestamp: number;
  data: string;
}
```

Getting data by comparing timestamps

Currently, the synchronizing strategy is one-way, from the server to the client. So what we need to do is simple: we compare the timestamps; if the server has the newer one, it responds with data and the server-side timestamp; otherwise, it responds with `undefined`:

```
class Server {
  store: DataStore = {
    timestamp: 0,
    data: ''
  };

  getData(clientTimestamp: number): DataStore {
    if (clientTimestamp < this.store.timestamp) {
      return this.store;
    } else {
      return undefined;
```

```
      }
    }
  }
```

Now we have provided a simple API for the client, and it's time to implement the client:

```
import { Server, DataStore } from './';

export class Client {
  store: DataStore = {
    timestamp: 0,
    data: undefined
  };
  constructor(
    public server: Server
  ) { }
}
```

Prefixing a `constructor` parameter with access modifiers (including `public`, `private`, and `protected`) will create a property with the same name and corresponding accessibility. It will also assign the value automatically when the constructor is called.

Now we need to add a `synchronize` method to the `Client` class that does the job:

```
synchronize(): void {
  let updatedStore = this.server.getData(this.store.timestamp);
  if (updatedStore) {
    this.store = updatedStore;
  }
}
```

That's easily done. However, are you already feeling somewhat awkward with what we've written?

Two-way synchronizing

Usually, when we talk about synchronization, we get updates from the server and push changes to the server as well. Now we are going to do the second part, pushing the changes if the client has newer data.

But first, we need to give the client the ability to update its data by adding an `update` method to the `Client` class:

```
update(data: string): void {
  this.store.data = data;
  this.store.timestamp = Date.now();
}
```

And we need the server to have the ability to receive data from the client as well. So we rename the `getData` method of the `Server` class as `synchronize` and make it satisfy the new job:

```
synchronize(clientDataStore: DataStore): DataStore {
  if (clientDataStore.timestamp > this.store.timestamp) {
    this.store = clientDataStore;
    return undefined;
  } else if (clientDataStore.timestamp < this.store.timestamp) {
    return this.store;
  } else {
    return undefined;
  }
}
```

Now we have the basic implementation of our synchronizing service. Later, we'll keep adding new things and make it capable of dealing with a variety of scenarios.

Things that went wrong while implementing the basics

Currently, what we've written is just too simple to be wrong. But there are still some semantic issues.

Passing a data store from the server to the client does not make sense

We used `DataStore` as the return type of the `synchronize` method on `Server`. But what we were actually passing through is not a data store, but information that involves data and its timestamp. The information object just *happened to* have the same properties as a data store *at this point in time*.

Also, it will be misleading to people who will later read your code (including yourself in the future). Most of the time, we are trying to eliminate redundancies. But that does not have to mean everything that looks the same. So let's make it two interfaces:

```
interface DataStore {
  timestamp: number;
  data: string;
}

interface DataSyncingInfo {
  timestamp: number;
  data: string;
}
```

I would even prefer to create another instance, instead of directly returning `this.store`:

```
return {
  timestamp: this.store.timestamp,
  data: this.store.data
};
```

However, if two pieces of code with different semantic meanings are doing the same thing from the perspective of code itself, you may consider extracting that part as a utility.

Making the relationships clear

Now we have two separated interfaces, `DataStore` and `DataSyncingInfo`, in `server.ts`. Obviously, `DataSyncingInfo` should be a shared interface between the server and the client, while `DataStore` happens to be the same on both sides, but it's not actually shared.

So what we are going to do is to create a separate `shared.d.ts` (it could also be `shared.ts` if it contains more than `typings`) that exports `DataSyncingInfo` and add another `DataStore` to `client.ts`.

 Do not follow this blindly. Sometimes it is designed for the server and the client to have exactly the same stores. If that's the situation, the interface should be shared.

Growing features

What we've done so far is basically useless. But, from now on, we will start to add features and make it capable of fitting in practical needs, including the capability of synchronizing multiple data items with multiple clients, and merging conflicts.

Synchronizing multiple items

Ideally, the data we need to synchronize will have a lot of items contained. Directly changing the type of `data` to an array would work if there were only very limited number of these items.

Simply replacing data type with an array

Now let's change the type of the `data` property of `DataStore` and `DataSyncingInfo` interfaces to `string[]`. With the help of TypeScript, you will get errors for unmatched types this change would cause. Fix them by annotating the correct types.

But obviously, this is far from an efficient solution.

Server-centered synchronization

If the data store contains a lot of data, the ideal approach would be only updating items that are not up-to-date.

For example, we can create a timestamp for every single item and send these timestamps to the server, then let the server decide whether a specific data item is up-to-date. This is a viable approach for certain scenarios, such as checking updates for software extensions. It is okay to occasionally send even hundreds of timestamps with item IDs on a fast network, but we are going to use another approach for different scenarios, or I won't have much to write.

User data synchronization of offline apps on a mobile phone is what we are going to deal with, which means we need to try our best to avoid wasting network resources.

 Here is an interesting question. What are the differences between user data synchronization and checking extension updates? Think about the size of data, issues with multiple devices, and more.

The reason why we thought about sending timestamps of all items is for the server to determine whether certain items need to be updated. However, is it necessary to have the timestamps of all data items stored on the client side?

What if we choose not to store the timestamp of data changing, but of data being synchronized with the server? Then we can get everything up-to-date by only sending the timestamp of the last successful synchronization. The server will then compare this timestamp with the last modified timestamps of all data items and decide how to respond.

As the title of this part suggests, the process is server-centered and relies on the server to generate the timestamps (though it does not have to, and practically should not, be the stamp of the actual time).

If you are getting confused about how these timestamps work, let's try again. The server will store the timestamps of the last time items were synchronized, and the client will store the timestamp of the last successful synchronization with the server. Thus, if no item on the server has a later timestamp than the client, then there's no change to the server data store after that timestamp. But if there are some changes, by comparing the timestamp of the client with the timestamps of server items, we'll know which items are newer.

Synchronizing from the server to the client

Now there seems to be quite a lot to change. Firstly, let's handle synchronizing data from server to client.

This is what's expected to happen on the server side:

- Add a timestamp and identity to every data item on the server
- Compare the client timestamp with every data item on the server

We don't need to actually compare the client timestamp with every item on server if those items have a sorted index. The performance would be acceptable using a database with a sorted index.

- Respond with items newer than what the client has as well as a new timestamp.

And here's what's expected to happen on the client side:

- Synchronize with the last timestamp sent to the server
- Update the local store with new data responded by the server
- Update the local timestamp of the last synchronization if it completes without error

Updating interfaces

First of all, we have now an updated data store on both sides. Starting with the server, the data store now contains an array of data items. So let's define the `ServerDataItem` interface and update `ServerDataStore` as well:

```
export interface ServerDataItem {
  id: string;
  timestamp: number;
  value: string;
}

export interface ServerDataStore {
  items: {
    [id: string]: ServerDataItem;
  };
}
```

 The `{ [id: string]: ServerDataItem }` type describes an object with `id` of type `string` as a key and has the value of type `ServerDataItem`. Thus, an item of type `ServerDataItem` can be accessed by `items['the-id']`.

And for the client, we now have different data items and a different store. The response contains only a subset of all data items, so we need IDs and a map with ID as the index to store the data:

```
export interface ClientDataItem {
  id: string;
  value: string;
}

export interface ClientDataStore {
  timestamp: number;
  items: {
    [id: string]: ClientDataItem;
  };
}
```

Previously, the client and server were sharing the same `DataSyncingInfo`, but that's going to change. As we'll deal with server-to-client synchronizing first, we care only about the timestamp in a synchronizing request for now:

```
export interface SyncingRequest {
  timestamp: number;
}
```

As for the response from the server, it is expected to have an updated timestamp with data items that have changed compared to the request timestamp:

```
export interface SyncingResponse {
  timestamp: number;
    changes: {
      [id: string]: string;
    };
}
```

I prefixed those interfaces with *Server* and *Client* for better differentiation. But it's not necessary if you are not exporting everything from `server.ts` and `client.ts` (in `index.ts`).

Updating the server side

With well-defined data structures, it should be pretty easy to achieve what we expected. To begin with, we have the `synchronize` method, which accepts a `SyncingRequest` and returns a `SyncingResponse`; and we need to have the updated timestamp as well:

```
synchronize(request: SyncingRequest): SyncingResponse {
  let lastTimestamp = request.timestamp;
  let now = Date.now();
  let serverChanges: ServerChangeMap = Object.create(null);
  return {
    timestamp: now,
    changes: serverChanges
  };
}
```

For the `serverChanges` object, `{}` (an object literal) might be the first thing (if not an ES6 Map) that comes to mind. But it's not absolutely safe to do so, because it would refuse `__proto__` as a key. The better choice would be `Object.create(null)`, which accepts all strings as its key.

Now we are going to add items that are newer than the client to `serverChanges`:

```
let items = this.store.items;

for (let id of Object.keys(items)) {
  let item = items[id];
  if (item.timestamp > lastTimestamp) {
    serverChanges[id] = item.value;
  }
}
```

Updating the client side

As we've changed the type of `items` under `ClientDataStore` to a map, we need to fix the initial value:

```
store: ClientDataStore = {
  timestamp: 0,
  items: Object.create(null)
};
```

Now let's update the `synchronize` method. Firstly, the client is going to send a request with a timestamp and get a response from the server:

```
synchronize(): void {
  let store = this.store;
  let response = this.server.synchronize({
    timestamp: store.timestamp
  });
}
```

Then we'll save the newer data items to the store:

```
let clientItems = store.items;
let serverChanges = response.changes;

for (let id of Object.keys(serverChanges)) {
  clientItems[id] = {
    id,
    value: serverChanges[id]
  };
}
```

Finally, update the timestamp of the last successful synchronization:

```
clientStore.timestamp = response.timestamp;
```

Updating the synchronization timestamp should be the last thing to do during a complete synchronization process. Make sure it's not stored earlier than data items, or you might have a broken offline copy if there's any errors or interruptions during synchronizing in the future.

 To ensure that this works as expected, an operation with the same change information should give the same results even if it's applied multiple times.

Synchronizing from client to server

For a server-centered synchronizing process, most of the changes are made through clients. Consequently, we need to figure out how to organize these changes before sending them to the server.

One single client only cares about its own copy of data. What difference would this make when comparing to the process of synchronizing data from the server to clients? Well, think about why we need the timestamp of every data item on the server in the first place. We need them because we want to know which items are new compared to a specific client.

Now, for changes on a client: if they ever happen, they need to be synchronized to the server without requiring specific timestamps for comparison.

However, we might have more than one client with changes that need to be synchronized, which means that changes made later in time might actually get synchronized earlier, and thus we'll have to resolve conflicts. To achieve that, we need to add the last modified time back to every data item on the server and the changed items on the client.

I've mentioned that the timestamps stored on the server for finding out what needs to be synchronized to a client do not need to be (and better not be) an actual stamp of a physical time point. For example, it could be the count of synchronizations that happened between all clients and the server.

Updating the client side

To handle this efficiently, we may create a separated map with the IDs of the data items that have changed as keys and the last modified time as the value in `ClientDataStore`:

```
export interface ClientDataStore {
  timestamp: number;
  items: {
    [id: string]: ClientDataItem;
  };
```

```
changed: {
  [id: string]: number;
};
}
```

You may also want to initialize its value as `Object.create(null)`.

Now when we update an item in the client store, we add the last modified time to the `changed` map as well:

```
update(id: string, value: string): void {
  let store = this.store;
  store.items[id] = {
    id,
    value
  };
  store.changed[id] = Date.now();
}
```

A single timestamp in `SyncingRequest` certainly won't do the job any more; we need to add a place for the changed data, a map with data item ID as the index, and the changed information as the value:

```
export interface ClientChange {
  lastModifiedTime: number;
  value: string;
}

export interface SyncingRequest {
  timestamp: number;
  changes: {
    [id: string]: ClientChange;
  };
}
```

Here comes another problem. What if a change made to a client data item is done offline, with the system clock being at the wrong time? Obviously, we need some time calibration mechanisms. However, there's no way to make perfect calibration. We'll make some assumptions so we don't need to start another chapter for time calibration:

- The system clock of a client may be late or early compared to the server. But it ticks at a normal speed and won't jump between times.
- The request sent from a client reaches the server in a relatively short time.

With those assumptions, we can add those building blocks to the client-side `synchronize` method:

1. Add client-side changes to the synchronizing request (of course, before sending it to the server):

```
let clientItems = store.items;
let clientChanges: ClientChangeMap = Object.create(null);

let changedTimes = store.changed;

for (let id of Object.keys(changedTimes)) {
  clientChanges[id] = {
    lastModifiedTime: changedTimes[id],
    value: clientItems[id].value
  };
}
```

2. Synchronize changes to the server with the current time of the client's clock:

```
let response = this.server.synchronize({
  timestamp: store.timestamp,
  clientTime: Date.now(),
  changes: clientChanges
});
```

3. Clean the changes after a successful synchronization:

```
store.changed = Object.create(null);
```

Updating the server side

If the client is working as expected, it should send synchronizing requests with changes. It's time to enable the server to handling those changes from the client.

There are going to be two steps for the server-side synchronization process:

1. Apply the client changes to server data store.
2. Prepare the changes that need to be synchronized to the client.

First, we need to add `lastModifiedTime` to server-side data items, as we mentioned before:

```
export interface ServerDataItem {
    id: string;
    timestamp: number;
    lastModifiedTime: number;
```

```
    value: string;
}
```

And we need to update the `synchronize` method:

```
let clientChanges = request.changes;
let now = Date.now();

for (let id of Object.keys(clientChanges)) {
  let clientChange = clientChanges[id];
  if (
    hasOwnProperty.call(items, id) &&
    items[id].lastModifiedTime > clientChange.lastModifiedTime
  ) {
    continue;
  }
  items[id] = {
    id,
    timestamp: now,
    lastModifiedTime,
    value: clientChange.value
  };
}
```

 We can actually use the `in` operator instead of `hasOwnProperty` here because the `items` object is created with `null` as its prototype. But a reference to `hasOwnProperty` will be your friend if you are using objects created by object literals, or in other ways, such as maps.

We already talked about resolving conflicts by comparing the last modified times. At the same time, we've made assumptions so we can calibrate the last modified times from the client easily by passing the client time to the server while synchronizing.

What we are going to do for calibration is to calculate the offset of the client time compared to the server time. And that's why we made the second assumption: the request needs to easily reach the server in a relatively short time. To calculate the offset, we can simply subtract the client time from the server time:

```
let clientTimeOffset = now - request.clientTime;
```

 To make the time calibration more accurate, we would want the earliest timestamp after the request hits the server to be recorded as "now". So in practice, you might want to record the timestamp of the request hitting the server before start processing everything. For example, for HTTP request, you may record the timestamp once the TCP connection gets established.

And now, the calibrated time of a client change is the sum of the original time and the offset. We can now decide whether to keep or ignore a change from the client by comparing the calibrated last modified time. It is possible for the calibrated time to be greater than the server time; you can choose either to use the server time as the maximum value or accept a small inaccuracy. Here, we will go the simple way:

```
let lastModifiedTime = Math.min(
  clientChange.lastModifiedTime + clientTimeOffset,
  now
);

if (
  hasOwnProperty.call(items, id) &&
  items[id].lastModifiedTime > lastModifiedTime
) {
  continue;
}
```

To make this actually work, we need to also exclude changes from the server that conflict with client changes in `SyncingResponse`. To do so, we need to know what the changes are that survive the conflict resolving process. A simple way is to exclude items with timestamp that equals `now`:

```
for (let id of Object.keys(items)) {
  let item = items[id];
  if (
    item.timestamp > lastTimestamp &&
    item.timestamp !== now
  ) {
    serverChanges[id] = item.value;
  }
}
```

So now we have implemented a complete synchronization logic with the ability to handle simple conflicts in practice.

Synchronizing multiple types of data

At this point, we've hard coded the data with the `string` type. But usually we will need to store varieties of data, such as numbers, booleans, objects, and so on.

If we were writing JavaScript, we would not actually need to change anything, as the implementation does not have anything to do with certain data types. In TypeScript, we don't need to do much either: just change the type of every related `value` to `any`. But that means you are losing type safety, which would definitely be okay if you are happy with that.

But taking my own preferences, I would like every variable, parameter, and property to be typed if it's possible. So we may still have a data item with `value` of type `any`:

```
export interface ClientDataItem {
  id: string;
  value: any;
}
```

We can also have derived interfaces for specific data types:

```
export interface ClientStringDataItem extends ClientDataItem {
  value: string;
}

export interface ClientNumberDataItem extends ClientDataItem {
  value: number;
}
```

But this does not seem to be good enough. Fortunately, TypeScript provides *generics*, so we can rewrite the preceding code as follows:

```
export interface ClientDataItem<T> {
  id: string;
  value: T;
}
```

Assuming we have a store that accepts multiple types of data items – for example, number and string – we can declare it as follows with the help of the `union` type:

```
export interface ClientDataStore {
  items: {
    [id: string]: ClientDataItem<number | string>;
  };
}
```

If you remember that we are doing something for offline mobile apps, you might be questioning the long property names in changes such as `lastModifiedTime`. This is a fair question, and an easy fix is to use `tuple` types, maybe along with `enums`:

```
const enum ClientChangeIndex {
  lastModifiedType,
  value
}

type ClientChange<T> = [number, T];

let change: ClientChange<string> = [0, 'foo'];
let value = change[ClientChangeIndex.value];
```

You can apply less or more of the typing things we are talking about depending on your preferences. If you are not familiar with them yet, you can read more here: `http://www.typescriptlang.org/handbook`.

Supporting multiple clients with incremental data

Making the typing system happy with multiple data types is easy. But in the real world, we don't resolve conflicts of all data types by simply comparing the last modified times. An example is counting the daily active time of a user cross devices.

It's quite clear that we need to have every piece of active time in a day on multiple devices summed up. And this is how we are going to achieve that:

1. Accumulate active durations between synchronizations on the client.
2. Add a UID (unique identifier) to every piece of time before synchronizing with the server.
3. Increase the server-side value if the UID does not exist yet, and then add the UID to that data item.

But before we actually get our hands on those steps, we need a way to distinguish incremental data items from normal ones, for example, by adding a `type` property.

As our synchronizing strategy is server-centered, related information is only required for synchronizing requests and conflict merging. Synchronizing responses does not need to include the details of changes, but just merged values.

I will stop telling how to update every interface step by step as we are approaching the final structure. But if you have any problems with that, you can check out the complete code bundle for inspiration.

Updating the client side

First of all, we need the client to support incremental changes. And if you've thought about this, you might already be confused about where to put the extra information, such as UIDs.

This is because we were mixing up the concept *change* (noun) with *value*. It was not a problem before because, besides the last modified time, the value is what a change is about. We used a simple map to store the last modified times and kept the store clean from redundancy, which balanced well under that scenario.

But now we need to distinguish between these two concepts:

- **Value**: a value describes what a data item is in a static way
- **Change**: a change describes the information that may transform the value of a data item from one to another

We need to have a general type of changes as well as a new data structure for incremental changes with a numeric value:

```
type DataType = 'value' | 'increment';

interface ClientChange {
  type: DataType;
}

interface ClientValueChange<T> extends ClientChange {
  type: 'value';
  lastModifiedTime: number;
  value: T;
}

interface ClientIncrementChange extends ClientChange {
  type: 'increment';
  uid: string;
  increment: number;
}
```

We are using the `string literal` type here, which was introduced in TypeScript 1.8. To learn more, please refer to the TypeScript handbook as we mentioned before.

Similar changes to the data store structure should be made. And when we update an item on the client side, we need to apply the correct operations based on different data types:

```
update(id: string, type: 'increment', increment: number): void;
update<T>(id: string, type: 'value', value: T): void;
update<T>(id: string, type: DataType, value: T): void;
update<T>(id: string, type: DataType, value: T): void {
  let store = this.store;
  let items = store.items;
  let storedChanges = store.changes;
  if (type === 'value') {
    // ...
  } else if (type === 'increment') {
    // ...
  } else {
    throw new TypeError('Invalid data type');
  }
}
```

Use the following code for normal changes (while `type` equals `'value'`):

```
let change: ClientValueChange<T> = {
  type: 'value',
  lastModifiedTime: Date.now(),
  value
};

storedChanges[id] = change;

if (hasOwnProperty.call(items, id)) {
  items[id].value = value;
} else {
  items[id] = {
    id,
    type,
    value
  };
}
```

For incremental changes, it takes a few more lines:

```
let storedChange = storedChanges[id] as ClientIncrementChange;

if (storedChange) {
  storedChange.increment += <any>value as number;
} else {
  storedChange = {
    type: 'increment',
    uid: Date.now().toString(),
    increment: <any>value as number
  };
  storedChanges[id] = storedChange;
}
```

 It's my personal preference to use `<T>` for `any` casting and `as  T` for non-any castings. Though it has been used in languages like C#, the `as` operator in TypeScript was originally introduced for compatibilities with XML tags in JSX. You can also write `<number><any>value` or `value as any as number` here if you like.

Don't forget to update the stored value. Just change = to += comparing to updating normal data items:

```
if (hasOwnProperty.call(items, id)) {
  items[id].value += value;
} else {
  items[id] = {
    id,
    type,
    value
  };
}
```

That's not hard at all. But hey, we see branches.

We are writing branches all the time, but what are the differences between branches such as `if (type === 'foo') { ... }` and branches such as `if (item.timestamp > lastTimestamp) { ... }`? Let's keep this question in mind and move on.

With necessary information added by the `update` method, we can now update the `synchronize` method of the client. But there is a flaw in practical scenarios: a synchronizing request is sent to the server successfully, but the client failed to receive the response from the server. In this situation, when `update` is called after a failed synchronization, the increment is added to the might-be-synchronized change (identified by its UID), which will be ignored by the server in future synchronizations. To fix this, we'll need to add a mark to all incremental changes that have started a synchronizing process, and avoid accumulating these changes. Thus, we need to create another change for the same data item.

This is actually a nice hint: as a change is about information that transforms a value from one to another, several changes pending synchronization might eventually be applied to one single data item:

```
interface ClientChangeList<T extends ClientChange> {
  type: DataType;
  changes: T[];
}

interface SyncingRequest {
  timestamp: number;
  changeLists: {
    [id: string]: ClientChangeList<ClientChange>;
  };
}

interface ClientIncrementChange extends ClientChange {
  type: 'increment';
  synced: boolean;
  uid: string;
  increment: number;
}
```

Now when we are trying to update an incremental data item, we need to get its last change from the change list (if any) and see whether it has ever been synchronized. If it has ever been involved in a synchronization, we create a new change instance. Otherwise, we'll just accumulate the increment property value of the last change on the client side:

```
let changeList = storedChangeLists[id];
let changes = changeList.changes;
let lastChange =
  changes[changes.length - 1] as ClientIncrementChange;

if (lastChange.synced) {
  changes.push({
    synced: false,
    uid: Date.now().toString(),
    increment: <any>value as number
  } as ClientIncrementChange);
} else {
  lastChange.increment += <any>value as number;
}
```

Or, if the change list does not exist yet, we'll need to set it up:

```
let changeList = {
  type: 'increment',
  changes: [
    {
      synced: false,
      uid: Date.now().toString(),
      increment: <any>value as number
    } as ClientIncrementChange
  ]
};

store.changeLists[id] = changeList;
```

We also need to update `synchronize` method to mark an incremental change as `synced` before starting the synchronization with the server. But the implementation is for you to do on your own.

Updating server side

Before we add the logic for handling incremental changes, we need to make server-side code adapt to the new data structure:

```
for (let id of Object.keys(clientChangeLists)) {
  let clientChangeList = clientChangeLists[id];
  let type = clientChangeList.type;
  let clientChanges = clientChangeList.changes;
  if (type === 'value') {
    // ...
  } else if (type === 'increment') {
    // ...
  } else {
    throw new TypeError('Invalid data type');
  }
}
```

The change list of a normal data item will always contain one and only one change. Thus we can easily migrate what we've written:

```
let clientChange = changes[0] as ClientValueChange<any>;
```

Now for incremental changes, we need to cumulatively apply possibly multiple changes in a single change list to a data item:

```
let item = items[id];
```

```
for (
  let clientChange
  of clientChanges as ClientIncrementChange[]
) {
  let {
    uid,
    increment
  } = clientChange;
  if (item.uids.indexOf(uid) < 0) {
    item.value += increment;
    item.uids.push(uid);
  }
}
```

But remember to take care of the timestamp or cases in which no item with a specified ID exists:

```
let item: ServerDataItem<any>;

if (hasOwnProperty.call(items, id)) {
  item = items[id];
  item.timestamp = now;
} else {
  item = items[id] = {
    id,
    type,
    timestamp: now,
    uids: [],
    value: 0
  };
}
```

Without knowing the current value of an incremental data item on the client, we cannot assure that the value is up to date. Previously, we decided whether to respond with a new value by comparing the timestamp with the timestamp of the current synchronization, but that does not work anymore for incremental changes.

A simple way to make this work is by deleting keys from `clientChangeLists` that still need to be synchronized to the client. And when preparing responses, it can skip IDs that are still in `clientChangeLists`:

```
if (
  item.timestamp > lastTimestamp &&
  !hasOwnProperty.call(clientChangeLists, id)
) {
  serverChanges[id] = item.value;
}
```

Remember to add `delete clientChangeLists[id];` for normal data items that did not survive conflicts resolving as well.

Now we have implemented a synchronizing logic that can do quite a lot jobs for offline applications. Earlier, I raised a question about increasing branches that do not look good. But if you know your features are going to end there, or at least with limited changes, it's not a bad implementation, although we'll soon cross the balance point, as meeting 80% of the needs won't make us happy enough.

Supporting more conflict merging

Though we have met the needs of 80%, there is still a big chance that we might want some extra features. For example, we want the ratio of the days marked as available by the user in the current month, and the user should be able to add or remove days from the list. We can achieve that in different ways, and we'll choose a simple way, as usual.

We are going to support synchronizing a set with operations such as add and remove, and calculate the ratio on the client.

New data structures

To describe set changes, we need a new `ClientChange` type. When we are adding or removing an element from a set, we only care about the last operation to the same element. This means that the following:

1. If multiple operations are made to the same element, we only need to keep the last one.
2. A `time` property is required for resolving conflicts.

So here are the new types:

```
enum SetOperation {
  add,
  remove
}

interface ClientSetChange extends ClientChange {
  element: number;
  time: number;
  operation: SetOperation;
}
```

The set data stored on the server side is going to be a little different. We'll have a map with the element (in the form of a `string`) as key, and a structure with `operation` and `time` properties as the values:

```
interface ServerSetElementOperationInfo {
  operation: SetOperation;
  time: number;
}
```

Now we have enough information to resolve conflicts from multiple clients. And we can generate the set by keys with a little help from the last operations done to the elements.

Updating client side

And now, the client-side `update` method gets a new part-time job: saving set changes just like value and incremental changes. We need to update the method signature for this new job (do not forget to add `'set'` to `DataType`):

```
update(
  id: string,
  type: 'set',
  element: number,
  operation: SetOperation
): void;
update<T>(
  id: string,
  type: DataType,
  value: T,
  operation?: SetOperation
): void;
```

We also need to add another `else if`:

```
else if (type === 'set') {
  let element = <any>value as number;
  if (hasOwnProperty.call(storedChangeLists, id)) {
    // ...
  } else {
    // ...
  }
}
```

If there are already operations made to this set, we need to find and remove that last operation to the target element (if any). Then append a new change with the latest operation:

```
let changeList = storedChangeLists[id];
let changes = changeList.changes as ClientSetChange[];

for (let i = 0; i < changes.length; i++) {
  let change = changes[i];
  if (change.element === element) {
    changes.splice(i, 1);
    break;
  }
}

changes.push({
  element,
  time: Date.now(),
  operation
});
```

If no change has been made since last successful synchronization, we'll need to create a new change list for the latest operation:

```
let changeList: ClientChangeList<ClientSetChange> = {
  type: 'set',
  changes: [
    {
      element,
      time: Date.now(),
      operation
    }
  ]
};

storedChangeLists[id] = changeList;
```

And again, do not forget to update the stored value. This is a little bit more than just assigning or accumulating the value, but it should still be quite easy to implement.

Updating the server side

Just like we've done with the client, we need to add a corresponding `else if` branch to merge changes of type `'set'`. We are also deleting the ID from `clientChangeLists` regardless of whether there are newer changes for a simpler implementation:

```
else if (type === 'set') {
  let item: ServerDataItem<{
    [element: string]: ServerSetElementOperationInfo;
  }>;
  delete clientChangeLists[id];
}
```

The conflict resolving logic is quite similar to what we do to the conflicts of normal values. We just need to make comparisons to each element, and only keep the last operation.

And when preparing the response that will be synchronized to the client, we can generate the set by putting together elements with `add` as their last operations:

```
if (item.type === 'set') {
  let operationInfos: {
    [element: string]: ServerSetElementOperationInfo;
  } = item.value;
  serverChanges[id] = Object
    .keys(operationInfos)
    .filter(element =>
      operationInfos[element].operation ===
        SetOperation.add
    )
    .map(element => Number(element));
} else {
  serverChanges[id] = item.value;
}
```

Finally, we have a working mess (if it actually works). Cheers!

Things that go wrong while implementing everything

When we started to add features, things were actually fine, if you are not obsessive about pursuing the feeling of design. Then we sensed the code being a little awkward as we saw more and more nested branches.

So now it's time to answer the question, what are the differences between the two kinds of branch we wrote? My understanding of why I am feeling awkward about the `if (type === 'foo') { ... }` branch is that it's not strongly related to the context. Comparing timestamps, on the other hand, is a more natural part of a certain synchronizing process.

Again, I am not saying this is bad. But this gives us a hint about where we might start our surgery from when we start to lose control (due to our limited brain capacity, it's just a matter of complexity).

Piling up similar yet parallel processes

Most of the code in this chapter is to handle the process of synchronizing data between a client and a server. To get adapted to new features, we just kept adding new things into methods, such as `update` and `synchronize`.

You might have already found that most outlines of the logic can be, and should be, shared across multiple data types. But we didn't do that.

If we look into what's written, the duplication is actually minor judging from the aspect of code texts. Taking the `update` method of the client, for example, the logic of every branch seems to differ. If finding abstractions has not become your built-in reaction, you might just stop there. Or if you are not a fan of long functions, you might refactor the code by splitting it into small ones of the same class. That could make things a little better, but far from enough.

Data stores that are tremendously simplified

In the implementation, we were playing heavily and directly with ideal *in-memory* stores. It would be nice if we could have a wrapper for it, and make the real store interchangeable.

This might not be the case for this implementation as it is based on extremely ideal and simplified assumptions and requirements. But adding a wrapper could be a way to provide useful helpers.

Getting things right

So let's get out of the illusion of comparing code one character at a time and try to find an abstraction that can be applied to updating all of these data types. There are two key points of this abstraction that have already been mentioned in the previous section:

- A `change` contains the information that can transform the value of an item from one to another
- Multiple changes could be generated or applied to one data item during a single synchronization

Now, starting from changes, let's think about what happens when an `update` method of a client is called.

Finding abstraction

Take a closer look to the method `update` of client:

- For data of the `'value'` type, first we create the change, including a new value, and then update the change list to make the newly created change the only one. After that, we update the value of data item.
- For data of the `'increment'` type, we add a change including the increment in the change list; or if a change that has not be synchronized already exists, update the increment of the existing change. And then, we update the value of the data item.
- Finally, for data of the `'set'` type, we create a change reflecting the latest operation. After adding the new change to the change list, we also remove changes that are no longer necessary. Then we update the value of the data item.

Things are getting clear. Here is what's happening to these data types when `update` is called:

1. Create new change.
2. Merge the new change to the change list.
3. Apply the new change to the data item.

Now it's even better. Every step is different for different data types, but different steps share the same outline; what we need to do is to implement different strategies for different data types.

Implementing strategies

Doing all kind of changes with a single `update` function could be confusing. And before we move on, let's split it into three different methods: `update` for normal values, `increase` for incremental values, and `addTo/removeFrom` for sets.

Then we are going to create a new private method called `applyChange`, which will take the change created by other methods and continue with step 2 and step 3. It accepts a strategy object with two methods: `append` and `apply`:

```
interface ClientChangeStrategy<T extends ClientChange> {
  append(list: ClientChangeList<T>, change: T): void;
  apply(item: ClientDataItem<any>, change: T): void;
}
```

For a normal data item, the strategy object could be as follows:

```
let strategy: ClientChangeStrategy<ClientValueChange<any>> = {
  append(list, change) {
    list.changes = [change];
  },
  apply(item, change) {
    item.value = change.value;
  }
};
```

And for incremental data item, it takes a few more lines. First, the `append` method:

```
let changes = list.changes;
let lastChange = changes[changes.length];

if (!lastChange || lastChange.synced) {
  changes.push(change);
} else {
  lastChange.increment += change.increment;
}
```

The `append` method is followed by the `apply` method:

```
if (item.value === undefined) {
  item.value = change.increment;
} else {
  item.value += change.increment;
}
```

Now in the `applyChange` method, we need to take care of the creation of non-existing items and change lists, and invoke different `append` and `apply` methods based on different data types.

The same technique can be applied to other processes. Though detailed processes that apply to the client and the server differ, we can still write them together as modules.

Wrapping stores

We are going to make a lightweight wrapper around plain in-memory store objects with the ability to read and write, taking the server-side store as an example:

```
export class ServerStore {
  private items: {
    [id: string]: ServerDataItem<any>;
  } = Object.create(null);
}

export class Server {
  constructor(
    public store: ServerStore
  ) { }
}
```

To fit our requirements, we need to implement `get`, `set`, and `getAll` methods (or even better, a `find` method with conditions) for `ServerStore`:

```
get<T, TExtra extends ServerDataItemExtra>(id: string):
  ServerDataItem<T> & TExtra {
  return hasOwnProperty.call(this.items, id) ?
    this.items[id] as ServerDataItem<T> & TExtra : undefined;
}

set<T, TExtra extends ServerDataItemExtra>(
  id: string,
  item: ServerDataItem<T> & Textra
): void {
  this.items[id] = item;
}

getAll<T, TExtra extends ServerDataItemExtra>():
  (ServerDataItem<T> & TExtra)[] {
  let items = this.items;
  return Object
    .keys(items)
```

```
        .map(id => items[id] as ServerDataItem<T> & TExtra);
}
```

You may have noticed from the interfaces and generics that I've also torn down `ServerDataItem` into intersection types of the common part and extras.

Summary

In this chapter, we've been part of the evolution of a simplified yet reality-related project. Starting with a simple code base that couldn't be wrong, we added a lot of features and experienced the process of putting acceptable changes together and making the whole thing a mess.

We were always trying to write readable code by either naming things nicely or adding semantically necessary redundancies, but that won't help much as the complexity grows.

During the process, we've learned how offline synchronizing works. And with the help of the most common design patterns, such as the Strategy Pattern, we managed to split the project into small and controllable parts.

In the upcoming chapters, we'll catalog more useful design patterns with code examples in TypeScript, and try to apply those design patterns to specific issues.

3
Creational Design Patterns

Creational design patterns in object-oriented programming are design patterns that are to be applied during the instantiation of objects. In this chapter, we'll be talking about patterns in this category.

Consider we are building a rocket, which has payload and one or more stages:

```
class Payload {
  weight: number;
}

class Engine {
  thrust: number;
}

class Stage {
  engines: Engine[];
}
```

In old-fashioned JavaScript, there are two major approaches to building such a rocket:

- Constructor with `new` operator
- Factory function

For the first approach, things could be like this:

```
function Rocket() {
  this.payload = {
    name: 'cargo ship'
  };
  this.stages = [
    {
      engines: [
        // ...
```

```
        ]
      }
    ];
  }

  var rocket = new Rocket();
```

And for the second approach, it could be like this:

```
function buildRocket() {
  var rocket = {};
  rocket.payload = {
    name: 'cargo ship'
  };
  rocket.stages = [
    {
      thrusters: [
        // ...
      ]
    }
  ];
  return rocket;
}

var rocket = buildRocket();
```

From a certain angle, they are doing pretty much the same thing, but semantically they differ a lot. The constructor approach suggests a strong association between the building process and the final product. The factory function, on the other hand, implies an interface of its product and claims the ability to build such a product.

However, neither of the preceding implementations provides the flexibility to modularly assemble rockets based on specific needs; this is what creational design patterns are about.

In this chapter, we'll cover the following creational patterns:

- **Factory method**: By using abstract methods of a factory instead of the constructor to build instances, this allows subclasses to change what's built by implementing or overriding these methods.
- **Abstract factory**: Defining the interface of compatible factories and their *products*. Thus by changing the factory passed, we can change the family of built products.
- **Builder**: Defining the *steps* of building complex objects, and changing what's built either by changing the sequence of steps, or using a different builder implementation.

- **Prototype**: Creating objects by cloning parameterized prototypes. Thus by replacing these prototypes, we may build different products.
- **Singleton**: Ensuring only one instance (under a certain scope) will be created.

It is interesting to see that even though the factory function approach to creating objects in JavaScript looks primitive, it does have parts in common with some patterns we are going to talk about (although applied to different scopes).

Factory method

Under some scenarios, a class cannot predict exactly what objects it will create, or its subclasses may want to create more specified versions of these objects. Then, the Factory Method Pattern can be applied.

The following picture shows the possible structure of the Factory Method Pattern applied to creating rockets:

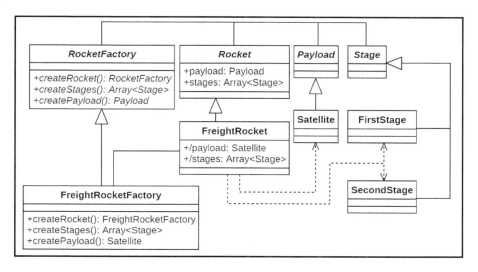

A **factory method** is a method of a factory that builds objects. Take building rockets as an example; a factory method could be a method that builds either the entire rocket or a single component. One factory method might rely on other factory methods to build its target object. For example, if we have a `createRocket` method under the `Rocket` class, it would probably call factory methods like `createStages` and `createPayload` to get the necessary components.

The Factory Method Pattern provides some flexibility upon reasonable complexity. It allows extendable usage by implementing (or overriding) specific factory methods. Taking `createStages` method, for example, we can create a one-stage rocket or a two-stage rocket by providing different `createStages` method that return one or two stages respectively.

Participants

The participants of a typical Factory Method Pattern implementation include the following:

- Product: `Rocket`

    Define an abstract class or an interface of a rocket that will be created as the product.

- Concrete product: `FreightRocket`

    Implement a specific rocket product.

- Creator: `RocketFactory`

    Define the optionally abstract factory class that creates products.

- Concrete creator: `FreightRocketFactory`

Implement or overrides specific factory methods to build products on demand.

Pattern scope

The Factory Method Pattern decouples `Rocket` from the constructor implementation and makes it possible for subclasses of a factory to change what's built accordingly. A concrete creator still cares about what exactly its components are and how they are built. But the implementation or overriding usually focuses more on each component, rather than the entire product.

Implementation

Let's begin with building a simple one-stage rocket that carries a 0-weight payload as the default implementation:

```
class RocketFactory {
```

```
buildRocket(): Rocket { }
createPayload(): Payload { }
createStages(): Stage[] { }
}
```

We start with creating components. We will simply return a payload with 0 weight for the factory method `createPayload` and one single stage with one single engine for the factory method `createStages`:

```
createPayload(): Payload {
  return new Payload(0);
}

createStages(): Stage[] {
  let engine = new Engine(1000);
  let stage = new Stage([engine]);
  return [stage];
}
```

After implementing methods to create the components of a rocket, we are going to put them together with the factory method `buildRocket`:

```
buildRocket(): Rocket {
  let rocket = new Rocket();
  let payload = this.createPayload();
  let stages = this.createStages();
  rocket.payload = payload;
  rocket.stages = stages;
  return rocket;
}
```

Now we have the blueprint of a simple rocket factory, yet with certain extensibilities. To build a rocket (that does nothing so far), we just need to instantiate this very factory and call its `buildRocket` method:

```
let rocketFactory = new RocketFactory();
let rocket = rocketFactory.buildRocket();
```

Next, we are going to build two-stage freight rockets that send satellites into orbit. Thus, there are some differences compared to the basic factory implementation.

First, we have a different payload, satellites, instead of a 0-weight placeholder:

```
class Satellite extends Payload {
  constructor(
    public id: number
  ) {
```

```
      super(200);
    }
  }
```

Second, we now have two stages, probably with different specifications. The first stage is going to have four engines:

```
class FirstStage extends Stage {
  constructor() {
    super([
      new Engine(1000),
      new Engine(1000),
      new Engine(1000),
      new Engine(1000)
    ]);
  }
}
```

While the second stage has only one:

```
class SecondStage extends Stage {
  constructor() {
    super([
      new Engine(1000)
    ]);
  }
}
```

Now we have what this new freight rocket would look like in mind, let's extend the factory:

```
type FreightRocketStages = [FirstStage, SecondStage];

class FreightRocketFactory extends RocketFactory {
  createPayload(): Satellite { }
  createStages(): FreightRocketStages { }
}
```

Here we are using the *type alias* of a *tuple* to represent the stages sequence of a freight rocket, namely the first and second stages. To find out more about type aliases, please refer to https://www.typescriptlang.org/doc s/handbook/advanced-types.html.

As we added the id property to Satellite, we might need a counter for each instance of the factory, and then create every satellite with a unique ID:

```
nextSatelliteId = 0;

createPayload(): Satellite {
```

```
    return new Satellite(this.nextSatelliteId++);
  }
```

Let's move on and implement the `createStages` method that builds first and second stage of the rocket:

```
createStages(): FreightRocketStages {
  return [
    new FirstStage(),
    new SecondStage()
  ];
}
```

Comparing to the original implementation, you may have noticed that we've automatically decoupled specific stage building processes from assembling them into constructors of different stages. It is also possible to apply another creational pattern for the initiation of every stage if it helps.

Consequences

In the preceding implementation, the factory method `buildRocket` handles the outline of the building steps. We were lucky to have the freight rocket in the same structure as the very first rocket we had defined.

But that won't always happen. If we want to change the class of products (`Rocket`), we'll have to override the entire `buildRocket` with everything else but the class name. This looks frustrating but it can be solved, again, by decoupling the creation of a rocket instance from the building process:

```
buildRocket(): Rocket {
  let rocket = this.createRocket();
  let payload = this.createPayload();
  let stages = this.createStages();
  rocket.payload = payload;
  rocket.stages = stages;
  return rocket;
}

createRocket(): Rocket {
  return new Rocket();
}
```

Thus we can change the rocket class by overriding the `createRocket` method. However, the return type of the `buildRocket` of a subclass (for example, `FreightRocketFactory`) is still `Rocket` instead of something like `FreightRocket`. But as the object created is actually an instance of `FreightRocket`, it is valid to cast the type by type assertion:

```
let rocket = FreightRocketFactory.buildRocket() as FreightRocket;
```

The trade-off is a little type safety, but that can be eliminated using generics. Unfortunately, in TypeScript what you get from a generic type argument is just a type without an actual value. This means that we may need another level of abstraction or other patterns that can use the help of type inference to make sure of everything.

The former option would lead us to the Abstract Factory Pattern.

 Type safety could be one reason to consider when choosing a pattern but usually, it will not be decisive. Please note we are not trying to switch a pattern for this single reason, but just exploring.

Abstract Factory

The Abstract Factory Pattern usually defines the interfaces of a collection of factory methods, without specifying concrete products. This allows an entire factory to be replaceable, in order to produce different products following the same production outline:

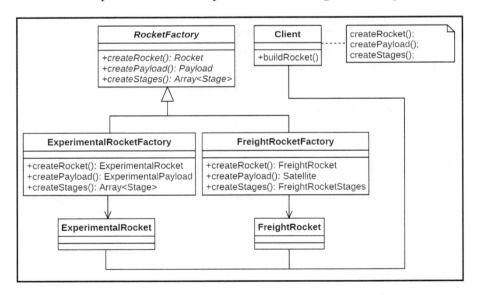

The details of the products (components) are omitted from the diagram, but do notice that these products belong to two parallel families: `ExperimentalRocket` and `FreightRocket`.

Different from the Factory Method Pattern, the Abstract Factory Pattern extracts another part called **client** that take cares of shaping the outline of the building process. This makes the factory part focused more on producing each component.

Participants

The participants of a typical Abstract Factory Pattern implementation include the following:

- **Abstract factory**: `RocketFactory`

  Defines the *industrial standards* of a factory which provide interfaces for manufacturing components or complex products.

- **Concrete factory**: `ExperimentalRocketFactory`, `FreightRocketFactory`

  Implements the interfaces defined by the abstract factory and builds concrete products.

- **Abstract products**: `Rocket`, `Payload`, `Stage[]`

  Define the interfaces of the products the factories are going to build.

- **Concrete products**: `ExperimentalRocket/FreightRocket`, `ExperimentalPayload/Satellite`, and so on.

  Presents actual products that are manufactured by a concrete factory.

- **Client**:

  Arranges the production process across factories (only if these factories conform to *industrial standards*).

Pattern scope

Abstract Factory Pattern makes the abstraction on top of different concrete factories. At the scope of a single factory or a single branch of factories, it just works like the Factory Method Pattern. However, the highlight of this pattern is to make a whole family of products interchangeable. A good example could be components of themes for a UI implementation.

Implementation

In the Abstract Factory Pattern, it is the client interacting with a concrete factory for building integral products. However, the concrete class of products is decoupled from the client during design time, while the client cares only about what a factory and its products look like instead of what exactly they are.

Let's start by simplifying related classes to interfaces:

```
interface Payload {
  weight: number;
}

interface Stage {
  engines: Engine[];
}

interface Rocket {
  payload: Payload;
  stages: Stage[];
}
```

And of course the abstract factory itself is:

```
interface RocketFactory {
  createRocket(): Rocket;
  createPayload(): Payload;
  createStages(): Stage[];
}
```

The building steps are abstracted from the factory and put into the client, but we still need to implement it anyway:

```
class Client {
  buildRocket(factory: RocketFactory): Rocket {
    let rocket = factory.createRocket();
    rocket.payload = factory.createPayload();
    rocket.stages = factory.createStages();
```

```
    return rocket;
  }
}
```

Now we have the same issue we previously had when we implemented the Factory Method Pattern. As different concrete factories build different rockets, the class of the product changes. However, now we have generics to the rescue.

First, we need a `RocketFactory` interface with a generic type parameter that describes a concrete rocket class:

```
interface RocketFactory<T extends Rocket> {
  createRocket(): T;
  createPayload(): Payload;
  createStages(): Stage[];
}
```

And second, update the `buildRocket` method of the client to support generic factories:

```
buildRocket<T extends Rocket>(
  factory: RocketFactory<T>
): T { }
```

Thus, with the help of the type system, we will have rocket type inferred based on the type of a concrete factory, starting with `ExperimentalRocket` and `ExperimentalRocketFactory`:

```
class ExperimentalRocket implements Rocket { }

class ExperimentalRocketFactory
implements RocketFactory<ExperimentalRocket> { }
```

If we call the `buildRocket` method of a client with an instance of `ExperimentalRocketFactory`, the return type will automatically be `ExperimentalRocket`:

```
let client = new Client();
let factory = new ExperimentalRocketFactory();
let rocket = client.buildRocket(factory);
```

Before we can complete the implementation of the `ExperimentalRocketFactory` object, we need to define concrete classes for the products of the family:

```
class ExperimentalPayload implements Payload {
  weight: number;
}
```

```
class ExperimentalRocketStage implements Stage {
  engines: Engine[];
}

class ExperimentalRocket implements Rocket {
  payload: ExperimentalPayload;
  stages: [ExperimentalRocketStage];
}
```

 Trivial initializations of payload and stage are omitted for more compact content. The same kinds of omission may be applied if they are not necessary for this book.

And now we may define the factory methods of this concrete factory class:

```
class ExperimentalRocketFactory
implements RocketFactory<ExperimentalRocket> {
  createRocket(): ExperimentalRocket {
    return new ExperimentalRocket();
  }
  createPayload(): ExperimentalPayload {
    return new ExperimentalPayload();
  }
  createStages(): [ExperimentalRocketStage] {
    return [new ExperimentalRocketStage()];
  }
}
```

Let's move on to another concrete factory that builds a freight rocket and products of its family, starting with the rocket components:

```
class Satellite implements Payload {
  constructor(
    public id: number,
    public weight: number
  ) { }
}

class FreightRocketFirstStage implements Stage {
  engines: Engine[];
}

class FreightRocketSecondStage implements Stage {
  engines: Engine[];
}

type FreightRocketStages =
```

```
[FreightRocketFirstStage, FreightRocketSecondStage];
```

Continue with the rocket itself:

```
class FreightRocket implements Rocket {
  payload: Satellite;
  stages: FreightRocketStages;
}
```

With the structures or classes of the freight rocket family defined, we are ready to implement its factory:

```
class FreightRocketFactory
implements RocketFactory<FreightRocket> {
  nextSatelliteId = 0;
  createRocket(): FreightRocket {
    return new FreightRocket();
  }
  createPayload(): Satellite {
    return new Satellite(this.nextSatelliteId++, 100);
  }
  createStages(): FreightRocketStages {
    return [
      new FreightRocketFirstStage(),
      new FreightRocketSecondStage()
    ];
  }
}
```

Now we once again have two families of rockets and their factories, and we can use the same client to build different rockets by passing different factories:

```
let client = new Client();

let experimentalRocketFactory = new ExperimentalRocketFactory();
let freightRocketFactory = new FreightRocketFactory();

let experimentalRocket =
  client.buildRocket(experimentalRocketFactory);

let freightRocket = client.buildRocket(freightRocketFactory);
```

Consequences

The Abstract Factory Pattern makes it easy and smooth to change the entire family of products. This is the direct benefit brought by the factory level abstraction. As a consequence, it also brings other benefits, as well as some disadvantages at the same time.

On the one hand, it provides better compatibility within the products in a specific family. As the products built by a single factory are usually meant to work together, we can assume that they tend to cooperate more easily.

But on the other hand, it relies on a common outline of the building process, although for a well-abstracted building process, this won't always be an issue. We can also parameterize factory methods on both concrete factories and the client to make the process more flexible.

Of course, an abstract factory does not have to be a pure interface or an abstract class with no methods implemented. An implementation in practice should be decided based on detailed context.

Although the Abstract Factory Pattern and Factory Method Pattern have abstractions of different levels, what they encapsulate are similar. For building a product with multiple components, the factories split the products into components to gain flexibility. However, a fixed family of products and their internal components may not always satisfy the requirements, and thus we may consider the Builder Pattern as another option.

Builder

While Factory Patterns expose the internal components (such as the payload and stages of a rocket), the Builder Pattern encapsulates them by exposing only the building steps and provides the final products directly. At the same time, the Builder Pattern also encapsulates the internal structures of a product. This makes it possible for a more flexible abstraction and implementation of building complex objects.

The Builder Pattern also introduces a new role called **director**, as shown in the following diagram. It is quite like the client in the Abstract Factory Pattern, although it cares only about build steps or pipelines:

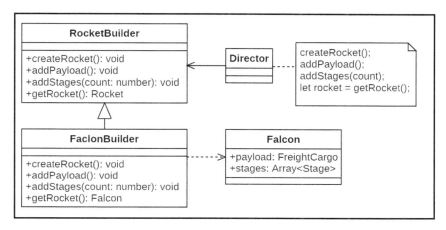

Now the only constraint from `RocketBuilder` that applies to a product of its subclass is the overall shape of a `Rocket`. This might not bring a lot of benefits with the `Rocket` interface we previously defined, which exposes some details of the rocket that the clients (by clients I mean those who want to send their satellites or other kinds of payload to space) may not care about that much. For these clients, what they want to know might just be which orbit the rocket is capable of sending their payloads to, rather than how many and what stages this rocket has.

Participants

The participants of a typical Builder Pattern implementation include the following:

- **Builder**: `RocketBuilder`

    Defines the interface of a builder that builds products.

- **Concrete builder**: `FalconBuilder`

    Implements methods that build parts of the products, and keeps track of the current building state.

- **Director**

    Defines the steps and collaborates with builders to build products.

- **Final product**: `Falcon`

    The product built by a builder.

Pattern scope

The Builder Pattern has a similar scope to the Abstract Factory Pattern, which extracts abstraction from a complete collection of operations that will finally initiate the products. Compared to the Abstract Factory Pattern, a builder in the Builder Pattern focuses more on the building steps and the association between those steps, while the Abstract Factory Pattern puts that part into the clients and makes its factory focus on producing components.

Implementation

As now we are assuming that stages are not the concern of the clients who want to buy rockets to carry their payloads, we can remove the `stages` property from the general `Rocket` interface:

```
interface Rocket {
  payload: Payload;
}
```

There is a rocket family called sounding rocket that sends probes to near space. And this means we don't even need to have the concept of stages. `SoundingRocket` is going to have only one `engine` property other than `payload` (which will be a `Probe`), and the only engine will be a `SolidRocketEngine`:

```
class Probe implements Payload {
  weight: number;
}

class SolidRocketEngine extends Engine { }

class SoundingRocket implements Rocket {
  payload: Probe;
  engine: SolidRocketEngine;
}
```

But still we need rockets to send satellites, which usually use `LiquidRocketEngine`:

```
class LiquidRocketEngine extends Engine {
  fuelLevel = 0;
  refuel(level: number): void {
    this.fuelLevel = level;
  }
}
```

And we might want to have the corresponding `LiquidRocketStage` abstract class that handles refuelling:

```
abstract class LiquidRocketStage implements Stage {
  engines: LiquidRocketEngine[] = [];
  refuel(level = 100): void {
    for (let engine of this.engines) {
      engine.refuel(level);
    }
  }
}
```

Now we can update `FreightRocketFirstStage` and `FreightRocketSecondStage` as subclasses of `LiquidRocketStage`:

```
class FreightRocketFirstStage extends LiquidRocketStage {
  constructor(thrust: number) {
    super();
    let enginesNumber = 4;
    let singleEngineThrust = thrust / enginesNumber;
    for (let i = 0; i < enginesNumber; i++) {
      let engine =
        new LiquidRocketEngine(singleEngineThrust);
      this.engines.push(engine);
    }
  }
}

class FreightRocketSecondStage extends LiquidRocketStage {
  constructor(thrust: number) {
    super();
    this.engines.push(new LiquidRocketEngine(thrust));
  }
}
```

The `FreightRocket` will remain the same as it was:

```
type FreightRocketStages =
  [FreightRocketFirstStage, FreightRocketSecondStage];
```

```
class FreightRocket implements Rocket {
  payload: Satellite;
  stages = [] as FreightRocketStages;
}
```

And, of course, there is the builder. This time, we are going to use an abstract class that has the builder partially implemented, with generics applied:

```
abstract class RocketBuilder<
  TRocket extends Rocket,
  TPayload extends Payload
> {
  createRocket(): void { }
  addPayload(payload: TPayload): void { }
  addStages(): void { }
  refuelRocket(): void { }
  abstract get rocket(): TRocket;
}
```

 There's actually no abstract method in this abstract class. One of the reasons is that specific steps might be optional to certain builders. By implementing no-op methods, the subclasses can just leave the steps they don't care about empty.

Here is the implementation of the Director class:

```
class Director {
  prepareRocket<
    TRocket extends Rocket,
    TPayload extends Payload
  >(
    builder: RocketBuilder<TRocket, TPayload>,
    payload: TPayload
  ): TRocket {
    builder.createRocket();
    builder.addPayload(payload);
    builder.addStages();
    builder.refuelRocket();
    return builder.rocket;
  }
}
```

 Be cautious, without explicitly providing a building context, the builder instance relies on the building pipelines being queued (either synchronously or asynchronously). One way to avoid risk (especially with asynchronous operations) is to initialize a builder instance every time you prepare a rocket.

Now it's time to implement concrete builders, starting with `SoundingRocketBuilder`, which builds a `SoundingRocket` with only one `SolidRocketEngine`:

```
class SoundingRocketBuilder
extends RocketBuilder<SoundingRocket, Probe> {
  private buildingRocket: SoundingRocket;
  createRocket(): void {
    this.buildingRocket = new SoundingRocket();
  }
  addPayload(probe: Probe): void {
    this.buildingRocket.payload = probe;
  }
  addStages(): void {
    let payload = this.buildingRocket.payload;
    this.buildingRocket.engine =
      new SolidRocketEngine(payload.weight);
  }
  get rocket(): SoundingRocket {
    return this.buildingRocket;
  }
}
```

There are several notable things in this implementation:

- The `addStages` method relies on the previously added payload to add an engine with the correct thrust specification.
- The `refuel` method is not overridden (so it remains no-op) because a solid rocket engine does not need to be refueled.

We've sensed a little about the context provided by a builder, and it could have a significant influence on the result. For example, let's take a look at `FreightRocketBuilder`. It could be similar to `SoundingRocket` if we don't take the `addStages` and `refuel` methods into consideration:

```
class FreightRocketBuilder
extends RocketBuilder<FreightRocket, Satellite> {
  private buildingRocket: FreightRocket;
  createRocket(): void {
    this.buildingRocket = new FreightRocket();
  }
  addPayload(satellite: Satellite): void {
    this.buildingRocket.payload = satellite;
  }
  get rocket(): FreightRocket {
    return this.buildingRocket;
  }
```

```
}
```

Assume that a payload that weighs less than 1000 takes only one stage to send into space, while payloads weighing more take two or more stages:

```
addStages(): void {
  let rocket = this.buildingRocket;
  let payload = rocket.payload;
  let stages = rocket.stages;
  stages[0] = new FreightRocketFirstStage(payload.weight * 4);
  if (payload.weight >= FreightRocketBuilder.oneStageMax) {
    stages[1] = FreightRocketSecondStage(payload.weight);
  }
}

static oneStageMax = 1000;
```

When it comes to refueling, we can even decide how much to refuel based on the weight of the payloads:

```
refuel(): void {
  let rocket = this.buildingRocket;
  let payload = rocket.payload;
  let stages = rocket.stages;
  let oneMax = FreightRocketBuilder.oneStageMax;
  let twoMax = FreightRocketBuilder.twoStagesMax;
  let weight = payload.weight;
  stages[0].refuel(Math.min(weight, oneMax) / oneMax * 100);
  if (weight >= oneMax) {
    stages[1]
      .refuel((weight - oneMax) / (twoMax - oneMax) * 100);
  }
}

static oneStageMax = 1000;
static twoStagesMax = 2000;
```

Now we can prepare different rockets ready to launch, with different builders:

```
let director = new Director();

let soundingRocketBuilder = new SoundingRocketBuilder();
let probe = new Probe();
let soundingRocket
  = director.prepareRocket(soundingRocketBuilder, probe);

let freightRocketBuilder = new FreightRocketBuilder();
let satellite = new Satellite(0, 1200);
```

```
let freightRocket
  = director.prepareRocket(freightRocketBuilder, satellite);
```

Consequences

As the Builder Pattern takes greater control of the product structures and how the building steps influence each other, it provides the maximum flexibility by subclassing the builder itself, without changing the director (which plays a similar role to a client in the Abstract Factory Pattern).

Prototype

As JavaScript is a prototype-based programming language, you might be using prototype related patterns all the time without knowing it.

We've talked about an example in the Abstract Factory Pattern, and part of the code is like this:

```
class FreightRocketFactory
implements RocketFactory<FreightRocket> {
  createRocket(): FreightRocket {
    return new FreightRocket();
  }
}
```

Sometimes we may need to add a subclass just for changing the class name while performing the same `new` operation. Instances of a single class usually share the same methods and properties, so we can `clone` one existing instance for new instances to be created. That is the concept of a prototype.

But in JavaScript, with the prototype concept built-in, `new Constructor()` does basically what a `clone` method would do. So actually a constructor can play the role of a concrete factory in some way:

```
interface Constructor<T> {
  new (): T;
}

function createFancyObject<T>(constructor: Constructor<T>): T {
  return new constructor();
}
```

With this privilege, we can parameterize product or component classes as part of other patterns and make creation even more flexible.

There is something that could easily be ignored when talking about the Prototype Pattern in JavaScript: cloning with the state. With the `class` syntax sugar introduced in ES6, which hides the prototype modifications, we may occasionally forget that we can actually modify prototypes directly:

```
class Base {
  state: number;
}

let base = new Base();
base.state = 0;

class Derived extends Base { }
Derived.prototype = base;

let derived = new Derived();
```

Now, the `derived` object will keep the `state` of the `base` object. This could be useful when you want to create copies of a specific instance, but keep in mind that properties in a prototype of these copies are not the *own properties* of these cloned objects.

Singleton

There are scenarios in which only one instance of the specific class should ever exist, and that leads to Singleton Pattern.

Basic implementations

The simplest singleton in JavaScript is an object literal; it provides a quick and cheap way to create a unique object:

```
const singleton = {
  foo(): void {
    console.log('bar');
  }
};
```

But sometimes we might want private variables:

```
const singleton = (() => {
  let bar = 'bar';
  return {
    foo(): void {
      console.log(bar);
    }
  };
})();
```

Or we want to take the advantage of an anonymous constructor function or class expression in ES6:

```
const singleton = new class {
  private _bar = 'bar';
  foo(): void {
    console.log(this._bar);
  }
} ();
```

 Remember that the `private` modifier only has an effect at compile time, and simply disappears after being compiled to JavaScript (although of course its accessibility will be kept in `.d.ts`).

However, it is possible to have the requirements for creating new instances of "singletons" sometimes. Thus a normal class will still be helpful:

```
class Singleton {
  bar = 'bar';
  foo(): void {
    console.log(bar);
  }
  private static _default: Singleton;

  static get default(): Singleton {
    if (!Singleton._default) {
      Singleton._default = new Singleton();
    }

    return Singleton._default;
  }
}
```

Another benefit brought by this approach is lazy initialization: the object only gets initialized when it gets accessed the first time.

Conditional singletons

Sometimes we might want to get "singletons" based on certain conditions. For example, every country usually has only one capital city, thus a capital city could be treated as a singleton under the scope of the specific country.

The condition could also be the result of context rather than explicit arguments. Assuming we have a class `Environment` and its derived classes, `WindowsEnvironment` and `UnixEnvironment`, we would like to access the correct environment singleton across platforms by using `Environment.default` and apparently, a selection could be made by the `default` getter.

For more complex scenarios, we might want a registration-based implementation to make it extendable.

Summary

In this chapter, we've talked about several important creational design patterns including the Factory Method, Abstract Factory, Builder, Prototype, and Singleton.

Starting with the Factory Method Pattern, which provides flexibility with limited complexity, we also explored the Abstract Factory Pattern, the Builder Pattern and the Prototype Pattern, which share similar levels of abstraction but focus on different aspects. These patterns have more flexibility than the Factory Method Pattern, but are more complex at the same time. With the knowledge of the idea behind each of the patterns, we should be able to choose and apply a pattern accordingly.

While comparing the differences, we also found many things in common between different creational patterns. These patterns are unlikely to be isolated from others and some of them can even collaborate with or complete each other.

In the next chapter, we'll continue to discuss structural patterns that help to form large objects with complex structures.

4
Structural Design Patterns

While creational patterns play the part of flexibly creating objects, structural patterns, on the other hand, are patterns about composing objects. In this chapter, we are going to talk about structural patterns that fit different scenarios.

If we take a closer look at structural patterns, they can be divided into *structural class patterns* and *structural object patterns*. Structural class patterns are patterns that play with "interested parties" themselves, while structural object patterns are patterns that weave pieces together (like Composite Pattern). These two kinds of structural patterns complement each other to some degree.

Here are the patterns we'll walk through in this chapter:

- **Composite**: Builds tree-like structures using primitive and composite objects. A good example would be the DOM tree that forms a complete page.
- **Decorator**: Adds functionality to classes or objects dynamically.
- **Adapter**: Provides a general interface and work with different adaptees by implementing different concrete adapters. Consider providing different database choices for a single content management system.
- **Bridge**: Decouples the abstraction from its implementation, and make both of them interchangeable.
- **Façade**: Provides a simplified interface for the combination of complex subsystems.
- **Flyweight**: Shares stateless objects that are being used many times to improve memory efficiency and performance.
- **Proxy**: Acts as the surrogate that takes extra responsibilities when accessing objects it manages.

Composite Pattern

Objects under the same class could vary from their properties or even specific subclasses, but a complex object can have more than just normal properties. Taking DOM elements, for example, all the elements are instances of class `Node`. These nodes form tree structures to represent different pages, but every node in these trees is complete and uniform compared to the node at the root:

```
<html>
  <head>
    <title>TypeScript</title>
  </head>
  <body>
    <h1>TypeScript</h1>
    <img />
  </body>
</html>
```

The preceding HTML represents a DOM structure like this:

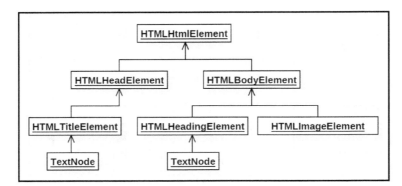

All of the preceding objects are instances of `Node`, they implement the interface of a *component* in Composite Pattern. Some of these nodes like HTML elements (except for `HTMLImageElement`) in this example have child nodes (components) while others don't.

Participants

The participants of Composite Pattern implementation include:

- **Component**: `Node`

    Defines the interface and implement the default behavior for objects of the composite. It should also include an interface to access and manage the child components of an instance, and optionally a reference to its parent.

- **Composite**: Includes some HTML elements, like `HTMLHeadElement` and `HTMLBodyElement`

    Stores child components and implements related operations, and of course its own behaviors.

- **Leaf**: `TextNode`, `HTMLImageElement`

    Defines behaviors of a primitive component.

- **Client**:

    Manipulates the composite and its components.

Pattern scope

Composite Pattern applies when objects can and should be abstracted recursively as components that form tree structures. Usually, it would be a natural choice when a certain structure needs to be formed as a tree, such as trees of view components, abstract syntax trees, or trees that represent file structures.

Implementation

We are going to create a composite that represents simple file structures and has limited kinds of components.

First of all, let's import related node modules:

```
import * as Path from 'path';
import * as FS from 'fs';
```

Module `path` and `fs` are built-in modules of Node.js, please refer to Node.js documentation for more information: `https://nodejs.org/api/`.

 It is my personal preference to have the first letter of a namespace (if it's not a function at the same time) in uppercase, which reduces the chance of conflicts with local variables. But a more popular naming style for namespace in JavaScript does not.

Now we need to make abstraction of the components, say `FileSystemObject`:

```
abstract class FileSystemObject {
  constructor(
    public path: string,
    public parent?: FileSystemObject
  ) { }

  get basename(): string {
    return Path.basename(this.path);
  }
}
```

We are using `abstract class` because we are not expecting to use `FileSystemObject` directly. An optional `parent` property is defined to allow us to visit the upper component of a specific object. And the `basename` property is added as a helper for getting the basename of the path.

The `FileSystemObject` is expected to have subclasses, `FolderObject` and `FileObject`. For `FolderObject`, which is a composite that may contain other folders and files, we are going to add an `items` property (getter) that returns other `FileSystemObject` it contains:

```
class FolderObject extends FileSystemObject {
  items: FileSystemObject[];

  constructor(path: string, parent?: FileSystemObject) {
    super(path, parent);
  }
}
```

We can initialize the `items` property in the `constructor` with actual files and folders existing at given `path`:

```
this.items = FS
  .readdirSync(this.path)
  .map(path => {
```

```
    let stats = FS.statSync(path);

    if (stats.isFile()) {
      return new FileObject(path, this);
    } else if (stats.isDirectory()) {
      return new FolderObject(path, this);
    } else {
      throw new Error('Not supported');
    }
  });
```

You may have noticed we are forming `items` with different kinds of objects, and we are also passing `this` as the `parent` of newly created child components.

And for `FileObject`, we'll add a simple `readAll` method that reads all bytes of the file:

```
  class FileObject extends FileSystemObject {
    readAll(): Buffer {
      return FS.readFileSync(this.path);
    }
  }
```

Currently, we are reading the child items inside a folder from the actual filesystem when a folder object gets initiated. This might not be necessary if we want to access this structure on demand. We may actually create a getter that calls `readdir` only when it's accessed, thus the object would act like a proxy to the real filesystem.

Consequences

Both the primitive object and composite object in Composite Pattern share the component interface, which makes it easy for developers to build a composite structure with fewer things to remember.

It also enables the possibility of using markup languages like XML and HTML to represent a really complex object with extreme flexibility. Composite Pattern can also make the rendering easier by having components rendered recursively.

As most components are compatible with having child components or being child components of their parents themselves, we can easily create new components that work great with existing ones.

Decorator Pattern

Decorator Pattern adds new functionality to an object dynamically, usually without compromising the original features. The word decorator in Decorator Pattern does share something with the word decorator in the ES-next decorator syntax, but they are not exactly the same. Classical Decorator Pattern as a phrase would differ even more.

The classical Decorator Pattern works with a composite, and the brief idea is to create decorators as components that do the decorating work. As composite objects are usually processed recursively, the decorator components would get processed automatically. So it becomes your choice to decide what it does.

The inheritance hierarchy could be like the following structure shown:

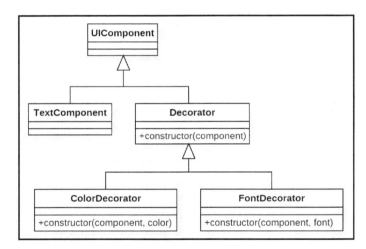

The decorators are applied recursively like this:

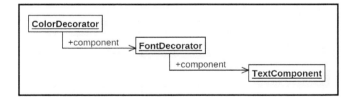

There are two prerequisites for the decorators to work correctly: the awareness of context or object that a decorator is decorating, and the ability of the decorators being applied. The Composite Pattern can easily create structures that satisfy those two prerequisites:

- The decorator knows what it decorates as the `component` property
- The decorator gets applied when it is rendered recursively

However, it doesn't really need to take a structure like a composite to gain the benefits from Decorator Pattern in JavaScript. As JavaScript is a dynamic language, if you can get your decorators called, you may add whatever you want to an object.

Taking method `log` under `console` object as an example, if we want a timestamp before every log, we can simply replace the `log` function with a wrapper that has the timestamp prefixed:

```
const _log = console.log;
console.log = function () {
  let timestamp = `[${new Date().toTimeString()}]`;
  return _log.apply(this, [timestamp, ...arguments]);
};
```

Certainly, this example has little to do with the classical Decorator Pattern, but it enables a different way for this pattern to be done in JavaScript. Especially with the help of new decorator syntax:

```
class Target {
  @decorator
  method() {
    // ...
  }
}
```

 TypeScript provides the decorator syntax transformation as an experimental feature. To learn more about decorator syntax, please check out the following link: `http://www.typescriptlang.org/docs/handbook/decorators.html`.

Participants

The participants of classical Decorator Pattern implementation include:

- **Component**: `UIComponent`

    Defines the interface of the objects that can be decorated.

- **ConcreteComponent**: `TextComponent`

  Defines additional functionalities of the concrete component.

- **Decorator**: `Decorator`

  Defines a reference to the component to be decorated, and manages the context. Conforms the interface of a component with proper behaviors.

- **ConcreteDecorator**: `ColorDecorator, FontDecorator`

  Defines additional features and exposes API if necessary.

Pattern scope

Decorator Pattern usually cares about objects, but as JavaScript is prototype-based, decorators would work well with the classes of objects through their prototypes.

The classical implementation of Decorator Pattern could have much in common with other patterns we are going to talk about later, while the function one seems to share less.

Implementation

In this part, we'll talk about two implementations of Decorator Pattern. The first one would be classical Decorator Pattern that decorates the target by wrapping with new classes that conform to the interface of `UIComponent`. The second one would be decorators written in new decorator syntax that processes target objects.

Classical decorators

Let's get started by defining the outline of objects to be decorated. First, we'll have the `UIComponent` as an abstract class, defining its abstract function `draw`:

```
abstract class UIComponent {
  abstract draw(): void;
}
```

Then a `TextComponent` that extends the `UIComponent`, as well as its text contents of class `Text`:

```
class Text {
  content: string;

  setColor(color: string): void { }
  setFont(font: string): void { }

  draw(): void { }
}

class TextComponent extends UIComponent {
  texts: Text[];

  draw(): void {
    for (let text of this.texts) {
      text.draw();
    }
  }
}
```

What's next is to define the interface of decorators to decorate objects that are instances of class `TextComponent`:

```
class Decorator extends UIComponent {
  constructor(
    public component: TextComponent
  ) {
    super();
  }

  get texts(): Text[] {
    return this.component.texts;
  }

  draw(): void {
    this.component.draw();
  }
}
```

Now we have everything for concrete decorators. In this example, `ColorDecorator` and `FontDecorator` look similar:

```
class ColorDecorator extends Decorator {
  constructor(
    component: TextComponent,
    public color: string
```

```
      ) {
        super(component);
      }

    draw(): void {
      for (let text of this.texts) {
        text.setColor(this.color);
      }

      super.draw();
    }
  }

  class FontDecorator extends Decorator {
    constructor(
      component: TextComponent,
      public font: string
    ) {
      super(component);
    }

    draw(): void {
      for (let text of this.texts) {
        text.setFont(this.font);
      }

      super.draw();
    }
  }
```

 In the implementation just described, `this.texts` in `draw` method calls the getter defined on class `Decorator`. As this in that context would ideally be an instance of class `ColorDecorator` or `FontDecorator`; the `texts` it accesses would finally be the array in its `component` property.

 This could be even more interesting or confusing if we have nested decorators like we will soon. Try to draw a schematic diagram if it confuses you later.

Now it's time to actually assemble them:

```
let decoratedComponent = new ColorDecorator(
  new FontDecorator(
    new TextComponent(),
    'sans-serif'
  ),
```

```
    'black'
);
```

The order of nesting decorators does not matter in this example. As either
`ColorDecorator` or `FontDecorator` is a valid `UIComponent`, they can be easily dropped
in and replace previous `TextComponent`.

Decorators with ES-next syntax

There is a limitation with classical Decorator Pattern that can be pointed out directly via its
nesting form of decorating. That applies to ES-next decorators as well. Take a look at the
following example:

```
class Foo {
  @prefix
  @suffix
  getContent(): string {
    return '...';
  }
}
```

What follows the @ character is an expression that evaluates to a decorator.
While a decorator is a function that processes target objects, we usually
use higher-order functions to parameterize a decorator.

We now have two decorators `prefix` and `suffix` decorating the `getContent` method. It
seems that they are just parallel at first glance, but if we are going to add a prefix and suffix
onto the content returned, like what the name suggests, the procedure would actually be
recursive rather than parallel just like the classical implementation.

To make decorators cooperate with others as we'd expect, we need to handle things
carefully:

```
function prefix(
  target: Object,
  name: string,
  descriptor: PropertyDescriptor
): PropertyDescriptor {
  let method = descriptor.value as Function;

  if (typeof method !== 'function') {
    throw new Error('Expecting decorating a method');
  }
```

```
  return {
    value: function () {
      return '[prefix] ' + method.apply(this, arguments);
    },
    enumerable: descriptor.enumerable,
    configurable: descriptor.configurable,
    writable: descriptor.writable
  };
}
```

 In current ECMAScript decorator proposal, when decorating a method or property (usually with getter or setter), you will have the third argument passed in as the property descriptor.

 Check out the following link for more information about property descriptors: https://developer.mozilla.org/en-US/docs/Web/JavaScript/Reference/Global_Objects/Object/defineProperty.

The `suffix` decorator would be just like the `prefix` decorator. So I'll save the code lines here.

Consequences

The key to the Decorator Pattern is being able to add functionalities dynamically, and decorators are usually expected to play nice with each other. Those expectations of Decorator Pattern make it really flexible to form a customized object. However, it would be hard for certain types of decorators to actually work well together.

Consider decorating an object with multiple decorators just like the second example of implementation, would the decorating order matter? Or should the decorating order matter?

A properly written decorator should always work no matter where it is in the decorators list. And it's usually *preferred* that the decorated target behaves almost the same with decorators decorated in different orders.

Adapter Pattern

Adapter Pattern connects existing classes or objects with another existing client. It makes classes that are not designed to work together possible to cooperate with each other.

An adapter could be either a *class* adapter or an *object* adapter. A class adapter extends the adaptee class and exposes extra APIs that would work with the client. An object adapter, on the other hand, does not extend the adaptee class. Instead, it stores the adaptee as a dependency.

The class adapter is useful when you need to access protected methods or properties of the adaptee class. However, it also has some restrictions when it comes to the JavaScript world:

- The adaptee class needs to be extendable
- If the client target is an abstract class other than pure interface, you can't extend the adaptee class and the client target with the same adapter class without a *mixin*
- A single class with two sets of methods and properties could be confusing

Due to those limitations, we are going to talk more about object adapters. Taking browser-side storage for example, we'll assume we have a client working with storage objects that have both methods `get` and `set` with correct signatures (for example, a storage that stores data online through AJAX). Now we want the client to work with IndexedDB for faster response and offline usage; we'll need to create an adapter for IndexedDB that gets and sets data:

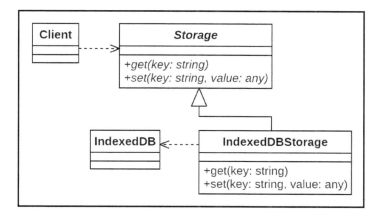

We are going to use Promise for receiving results or errors of asynchronous operations. See the following link for more information if you are not yet familiar with Promise: `https://d eveloper.mozilla.org/en-US/docs/Web/JavaScript/Reference/Global_Objects/Prom ise`.

Participants

The participants of Adapter Pattern include:

- **Target:** `Storage`

  Defines the interface of existing targets that works with client

- **Adaptee:** `IndexedDB`

  The implementation that is not designed to work with the client

- **Adapter:** `IndexedDBStorage`

  Conforms the interface of target and interacts with adaptee

- **Client.**

  Manipulates the target

Pattern scope

Adapter Pattern can be applied when the existing client class is not designed to work with the existing adaptees. It focuses on the unique *adapter* part when applying to different combinations of clients and adaptees.

Implementation

Start with the `Storage` interface:

```
interface Storage {
  get<T>(key: string): Promise<T>;
  set<T>(key: string, value: T): Promise<void>;
}
```

 We defined the `get` method with generic, so that if we neither specify the generic type, nor cast the value type of a returned Promise, the type of the value would be { }. This would probably fail following type checking.

With the help of examples found on MDN, we can now set up the IndexedDB adapter. Visit `IndexedDBStorage`: https://developer.mozilla.org/en-US/docs/Web/API/IndexedDB _API/Using_IndexedDB.

The creation of IndexedDB instances is asynchronous. We could put the opening operation inside a `get` or `set` method so the database can be opened on demand. But for now, let's make it easier by creating an instance of `IndexedDBStorage` that has a database instance which is already opened.

However, constructors usually don't have asynchronous code. Even if they do, it cannot apply changes to the instance before completing the construction. Fortunately, Factory Method Pattern works well with asynchronous initiation:

```
class IndexedDBStorage implements Storage {
  constructor(
    public db: IDBDatabase,
    public storeName = 'default'
  ) { }

  open(name: string): Promise<IndexedDBStorage> {
    return new Promise<IndexedDBStorage>(
      (resolve, reject) => {
      let request = indexedDB.open(name);
      // ...
    });
  }
}
```

Inside the Promise resolver of method `open`, we'll get the asynchronous work done:

```
let request = indexedDB.open(name);

request.onsuccess = event => {
  let db = request.result as IDBDatabase;
  let storage = new IndexedDBStorage(db);
  resolve(storage);
};

request.onerror = event => {
  reject(request.error);
};
```

Now when we are accessing an instance of IndexedDBStorage, we can assume it has an opened database and is ready to make queries. To make changes or to get values from the database, we need to create a transaction. Here's how:

```
get<T>(key: string): Promise<T> {
  return new Promise<T>((resolve, reject) => {
    let transaction = this.db.transaction(this.storeName);
    let store = transaction.objectStore(this.storeName);

    let request = store.get(key);

    request.onsuccess = event => {
      resolve(request.result);
    };

    request.onerror = event => {
      reject(request.error);
    };
  });
}
```

Method set is similar. But while the transaction is by default read-only, we need to explicitly specify 'readwrite' mode.

```
set<T>(key: string, value: T): Promise<void> {
  return new Promise<void>((resolve, reject) => {
    let transaction =
      this.db.transaction(this.storeName, 'readwrite');
    let store = transaction.objectStore(this.storeName);

    let request = store.put(value, key);

    request.onsuccess = event => {
      resolve();
    };

    request.onerror = event => {
      reject(request.error);
    };
  });
}
```

And now we can have a drop-in replacement for the previous storage used by the client.

Consequences

By applying Adapter Pattern, we can fill the gap between classes that originally would not work together. In this situation, Adapter Pattern is quite a straightforward solution that might come to mind.

But in other scenarios like a debugger *adapter* for debugging extensions of an IDE, the implementation of Adapter Pattern could be more challenging.

Bridge Pattern

Bridge Pattern decouples the abstraction manipulated by clients from functional implementations and makes it possible to add or replace these abstractions and implementations easily.

Take a set of *cross-API* UI elements as an example:

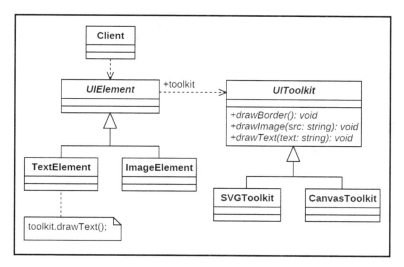

We have the abstraction UIElement that can access different implementations of UIToolkit for creating different UI based on either SVG or canvas. In the preceding structure, the *bridge* is the connection between UIElement and UIToolkit.

Participants

The participants of Bridge Pattern include:

- **Abstraction:** `UIElement`

    Defines the interface of objects to be manipulated by the client and stores the reference to its implementer.

- **Refined abstraction**: `TextElement`, `ImageElement`

    Extends abstraction with specialized behaviors.

- **Implementer**: `UIToolkit`

    Defines the interface of a general implementer that will eventually carry out the operations defined in abstractions. The implementer usually cares only about basic operations while the abstraction will handle high-level operations.

- **Concrete implementer**: `SVGToolkit`, `CanvasToolkit`

    Implements the implementer interface and manipulates low-level APIs.

Pattern scope

Although having abstraction and implementer decoupled provides Bridge Pattern with the ability to work with several abstractions and implementers, most of the time, bridge patterns work only with a single implementer.

If you take a closer look, you will find Bridge Pattern is extremely similar to Adapter Pattern. However, while Adapter Pattern tries to make existing classes cooperate and focuses on the adapters part, Bridge Pattern foresees the divergences and provides a well-thought-out and universal interface for its abstractions that play the part of adapters.

Implementation

A working implementation could be non-trivial in the example we are talking about. But we can still sketch out the skeleton easily.

Start with implementer `UIToolkit` and abstraction `UIElement` that are directly related to the bridge concept:

```
interface UIToolkit {
  drawBorder(): void;
  drawImage(src: string): void;
  drawText(text: string): void;
}

abstract class UIElement {
  constructor(
    public toolkit: UIToolkit
  ) { }

  abstract render(): void;
}
```

And now we can extend `UIElement` for refined abstractions with different behaviors. First the `TextElement`   class:

```
class TextElement extends UIElement {
  constructor(
    public text: string,
    toolkit: UIToolkit
  ) {
    super(toolkit);
  }

  render(): void {
    this.toolkit.drawText(this.text);
  }
}
```

And the `ImageElement` class with similar code:

```
class ImageElement extends UIElement {
  constructor(
    public src: string,
    toolkit: UIToolkit
  ) {
    super(toolkit);
  }

  render(): void {
    this.toolkit.drawImage(this.src);
  }
}
```

By creating concrete `UIToolkit` subclasses, we can manage to make everything together with the client. But as it could lead to hard work we would not want to touch now, we'll skip it by using a variable pointing to `undefined` in this example:

```
let toolkit: UIToolkit;

let imageElement = new ImageElement('foo.jpg', toolkit);
let textElement = new TextElement('bar', toolkit);

imageElement.render();
textElement.render();
```

In the real world, the render part could also be a heavy lift. But as it's coded at a relatively higher-level, it tortures you in a different way.

Consequences

Despite having completely different names for the abstraction (`UIElement`) in the example above and the adapter interface (`Storage`), they play similar roles in a static combination.

However, as we mentioned in the pattern scope section, the intentions of Bridge Pattern and Adapter Pattern differ.

By decoupling the abstraction and implementer, Bridge Pattern brings great extensibility to the system. The client does not need to know about the implementation details, and this helps to build more stable systems as it forms a healthier dependency structure.

Another bonus that might be brought by Bridge Pattern is that, with a properly configured build process, it can reduce compilation time as the compiler does not need to know information on the other end of the bridge when changes are made to a refined abstraction or concrete implementer.

Façade Pattern

The Façade Pattern organizes subsystems and provides a unified higher-level interface. An example that might be familiar to you is a modular system. In JavaScript (and of course TypeScript), people use modules to organize code. A modular system makes projects easier to maintain, as a clean project structure can help reveal the interconnections among different parts of the project.

It is common that one project gets referenced by others, but obviously the project that references other projects doesn't and shouldn't care much about the inner structures of its dependencies. Thus a façade can be introduced for a dependency project to provide a higher-level API and expose what really matters to its dependents.

Take a robot as an example. People who build a robot and its components will need to control every part separately and let them cooperate at the same time. However, people who want to use this robot would only need to send simple commands like "walk" and "jump".

For the most flexible usage, the robot "SDK" can provide classes like `MotionController`, `FeedbackController`, `Thigh`, `Shank`, `Foot` and so on. Possibly like the following image shows:

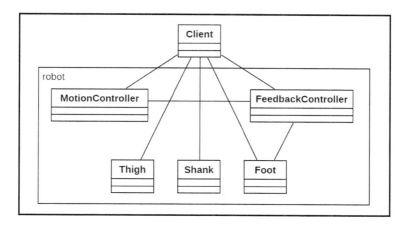

But certainly, most of the people who want to control or program this robot do not want to know as many details as this. What they really want is not a fancy tool box with *everything* inbox, but just an integral robot that follows their commands. Thus the robot "SDK" can actually provide a façade that controls the inner pieces and exposes much simpler APIs:

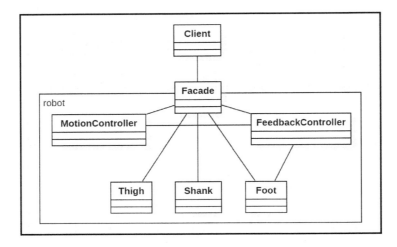

Unfortunately, Façade Pattern leaves us an open question of how to design the façade API and subsystems. Answering this question properly is not easy work.

Participants

The participants of a Façade Pattern are relatively simple when it comes to their categories:

- **Façade:** `Robot`

  Defines a set of higher-level interfaces, and makes subsystems cooperate.

- **Subsystems:** `MotionController`, `FeedbackController`, `Thigh`, `Shank` and `Foot`

  Implements their own functionalities and communicates internally with other subsystems if necessary. Subsystems are dependencies of a façade, and they do not depend on the façade.

Pattern scope

Façades usually act as junctions that connect a higher-level system and its subsystems. The key to the Façade Pattern is to draw a line between what a dependent should or shouldn't care about of its dependencies.

Implementation

Consider putting up a robot with its left and right legs, we can actually add another abstraction layer called Leg that manages Thigh, Shank , and Foot. If we are going to separate motion and feedback controllers to different legs respectively, we may also add those two as part of the Leg:

```
class Leg {
  thigh: Thigh;
  shank: Shank;
  foot: Foot;

  motionController: MotionController;
  feedbackController: FeedbackController;
}
```

Before we add more details to Leg, let's first define MotionController and FeedbackController .

The MotionController is supposed to control a whole leg based on a value or a set of values. Here we are simplifying that as a single angle for not being distracted by this impossible robot:

```
class MotionController {
  constructor(
    public leg: Leg
  ) { }

  setAngle(angle: number): void {
    let {
      thigh,
      shank,
      foot
    } = this.leg;

    // ...
  }
}
```

And the `FeedbackController` is supposed to be an instance of `EventEmitter` that reports the state changes or useful events:

```
import { EventEmitter } from 'events';

class FeedbackController extends EventEmitter {
  constructor(
    public foot: Foot
  ) {
    super();
  }
}
```

Now we can make class `Leg` relatively complete:

```
class Leg {
  thigh = new Thigh();
  shank = new Shank();
  foot = new Foot();

  motionController: MotionController;
  feedbackController: FeedbackController;

  constructor() {
    this.motionController =
      new MotionController(this);
    this.feedbackController =
      new FeedbackController(this.foot);

    this.feedbackController.on('touch', () => {
      // ...
    });
  }
}
```

Let's put two legs together to sketch the skeleton of a robot:

```
class Robot {
  leftLegMotion: MotionController;
  rightLegMotion: MotionController;

  leftFootFeedback: FeedbackController;
  rightFootFeedback: FeedbackController;

  walk(steps: number): void { }
  jump(strength: number): void { }
}
```

I'm omitting the definition of classes `Thigh`, `Shank` , and `Foot` as we are not actually going to walk the robot. Now for a user that only wants to walk or jump a robot via simple API, they can make it via the `Robot` object that has everything connected.

Consequences

Façade Pattern loosens the coupling between client and subsystems. Though it does not decouple them completely as you will probably still need to work with objects defined in subsystems.

Façades usually forward operations from client to proper subsystems or even do heavy work to make them work together.

With the help of Façade Pattern, the system and the relationship and structure within the system can stay clean and intuitive.

Flyweight Pattern

A flyweight in Flyweight Pattern is a stateless object that can be shared across objects or maybe classes many times. Obviously, that suggests Flyweight Pattern is a pattern about memory efficiency and maybe performance if the construction of objects is expensive.

Taking drawing snowflakes as an example. Despite real snowflakes being different to each other, when we are trying to draw them onto canvas, we usually have a limited number of styles. However, by adding *properties* like sizes and transformations, we can create a beautiful snow scene with limited snowflake styles.

As a flyweight is stateless, ideally it allows multiple operations simultaneously. You might need to be cautious when working with multi-thread stuff. Fortunately, JavaScript is usually single-threaded and avoids this issue if all related code is synchronous. You will still need to take care in detailed scenarios if your code is working asynchronously.

Assume we have some flyweights of class `Snowflake`:

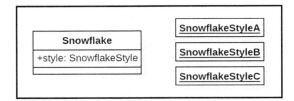

When it snows, it would look like this:

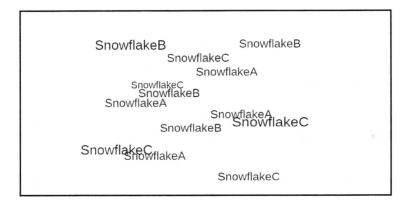

In the image above, snowflakes in different styles are the result of rendering with different properties.

It's common that we would have styles and image resources being loaded dynamically, thus we could use a `FlyweightFactory` for creating and managing flyweight objects.

Participants

The simplest implementation of Flyweight Pattern has the following participants:

- **Flyweight**: `Snowflake`

  Defines the class of flyweight objects.

- **Flyweight factory**: `FlyweightFactory`

  Creates and manages flyweight objects.

- **Client**.

    Stores states of targets and uses flyweight objects to manipulate these targets.

With these participants, we assume that the manipulation could be accomplished through flyweights with different states. It would also be helpful sometimes to have `concrete flyweight` class allowing customized behaviors.

Pattern scope

Flyweight Pattern is a result of efforts to improving memory efficiency and performance. The implementation cares about having the instances being stateless, and it is usually the client that manages detailed states for different targets.

Implementation

What makes Flyweight Pattern useful in the snowflake example is that a snowflake with the same style usually shares the same image. The image is what consumes time to load and occupies notable memory.

We are starting with a fake `Image` class that pretends to load images:

```
class Image {
  constructor(url: string) { }
}
```

The `Snowflake` class in our example has only a single `image` property, and that is a property that will be shared by many snowflakes to be drawn. As the instance is now stateless, parameters from context are required for rendering:

```
class Snowflake {
  image: Image;

  constructor(
    public style: string
  ) {
    let url = style + '.png';
    this.image = new Image(url);
  }

  render(x: number, y: number, angle: number): void {
    // ...
  }
```

```
  }
```

The flyweights are managed by a factory for easier accessing. We'll have a `SnowflakeFactory` that caches created snowflake objects with certain styles:

```typescript
const hasOwnProperty = Object.prototype.hasOwnProperty;

class SnowflakeFactory {
  cache: {
    [style: string]: Snowflake;
  } = {};

  get(style: string): Snowflake {
    let cache = this.cache;
    let snowflake: Snowflake;

    if (hasOwnProperty.call(cache, style)) {
      snowflake = cache[style];
    } else {
      snowflake = new Snowflake(style);
      cache[style] = snowflake;
    }

    return snowflake;
  }
}
```

With building blocks ready, we'll implement the client (`Sky`) that snows:

```typescript
const SNOW_STYLES = ['A', 'B', 'C'];

class Sky {
  constructor(
    public width: number,
    public height: number
  ) { }

  snow(factory: SnowflakeFactory, count: number) { }
}
```

We are going to fill the sky with random snowflakes at random positions. Before that let's create a helper function that generates a number between 0 and a max value given:

```typescript
function getRandomInteger(max: number): number {
  return Math.floor(Math.random() * max);
}
```

And then complete method `snow` of `Sky`:

```
snow(factory: SnowflakeFactory, count: number) {
    let stylesCount = SNOW_STYLES.length;

    for (let i = 0; i < count; i++) {
        let style = SNOW_STYLES[getRandomInteger(stylesCount)];
        let snowflake = factory.get(style);

        let x = getRandomInteger(this.width);
        let y = getRandomInteger(this.height);

        let angle = getRandomInteger(60);

        snowflake.render(x, y, angle);
    }
}
```

Now we may have thousands of snowflakes in the sky but with only three instances of `Snowflake` created. You can continue this example by storing the state of snowflakes and animating the snowing.

Consequences

Flyweight Pattern reduces the total number of objects involved in a system. As a direct result, it may save quite a lot memory. This saving becomes more significant when the flyweights get used by the client that processes a large number of targets.

Flyweight Pattern also brings extra logic into the system. When to use or not to use this pattern is again a balancing game between development efficiency and runtime efficiency from this point of view. Though most of the time, if there's not a good reason, we go with development efficiency.

Proxy Pattern

Proxy Pattern applies when the program needs to know about or to intervene the behavior of accessing objects. There are several detailed scenarios in Proxy Pattern, and we can distinguish those scenarios by their different purposes:

- **Remote proxy**: A proxy with interface to manipulate remote objects, such as data items on a remote server

- **Virtual proxy**: A proxy that manages expensive objects which need to be loaded on demand
- **Protection proxy**: A proxy that controls access to target objects, typically it verifies permissions and validates values
- **Smart proxy**: A proxy that does additional operations when accessing target objects

In the section of Adapter Pattern, we used factory method `open` that creates an object asynchronously. As a trade-off, we had to let the client wait before the object gets created.

With Proxy Pattern, we could now `open` database on demand and create storage instances synchronously.

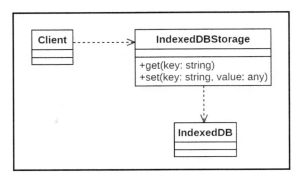

 A proxy is usually dedicated to object or objects with known methods and properties. But with the new `Proxy` API provided in ES6, we can get more interesting things done by getting to know what methods or properties are being accessed. Please refer to the following link for more information: `htt ps://developer.mozilla.org/en-US/docs/Web/JavaScript/Reference /Global_Objects/Proxy`.

Participants

The participants of Proxy Pattern include:

- **Proxy**: `IndexedDBStorage`

    Defines interface and implements operations to manage access to the subject.

- **Subject**: `IndexedDB`

  The subject to be accessed by proxy.

- **Client**: Accesses subject via proxy.

Pattern scope

Despite having a similar structure to Adapter Pattern, the key of Proxy Pattern is to intervene the access to target objects rather than to adapt an incompatible interface. Sometimes it might change the result of a specific method or the value of a certain property, but that is probably for falling back or exception handling purposes.

Implementation

There are two differences we'll have in this implementation compared to the example for pure Adapter Pattern. First, we'll create the `IndexedDBStorage` instance with a constructor, and have the database opened on demand. Second, we are going to add a useless permission checking for methods `get` and `set`.

Now when we call the method `get` or `set`, the database could either have been opened or not. Promise is a great choice for representing a value that might either be pending or settled. Consider this example:

```
let ready = new Promise<string>(resolve => {
  setTimeout(() => {
    resolve('biu~');
  }, Math.random() * 1000);
});

setTimeout(() => {
  ready.then(text => {
    console.log(text);
  });
}, 999);
```

It's hard to tell whether Promise `ready` is fulfilled when the second timeout fires. But the overall behavior is easy to predict: it will log the `'biu~'` text in around 1 second. By replacing the Promise variable `ready` with a method or getter, it would be able to start the asynchronous operation only when needed.

So let's start the refactoring of class `IndexedDBStorage` with the getter that creates the Promise of the database to be opened:

```
private dbPromise: Promise<IDBDatabase>;

constructor(
  public name: string,
  public storeName = 'default'
) { }

private get dbReady(): Promise<IDBDatabase> {
  if (!this.dbPromise) {
    this.dbPromise =
      new Promise<IDBDatabase>((resolve, reject) => {
      let request = indexedDB.open(name);

      request.onsuccess = event => {
        resolve(request.result);
      };

      request.onerror = event => {
        reject(request.error);
      };
    });
  }

  return this.dbPromise;
}
```

Now the first time we access property `dbReady`, it will open the database and create a Promise that will be fulfilled with the database being opened. To make this work with methods `get` and `set`, we just need to wrap what we've implemented into a `then` method following the `dbReady` Promise.

First for method `get`:

```
get<T>(key: string): Promise<T> {
  return this
    .dbReady
    .then(db => new Promise<T>((resolve, reject) => {
      let transaction = db.transaction(this.storeName);
      let store = transaction.objectStore(this.storeName);

      let request = store.get(key);

      request.onsuccess = event => {
        resolve(request.result);
```

```
        };

        request.onerror = event => {
          reject(request.error);
        };
      }));
  }
```

And followed by updated method `set`:

```
set<T>(key: string, value: T): Promise<void> {
  return this
    .dbReady
    .then(db => new Promise<void>((resolve, reject) => {
      let transaction = db
          .transaction(this.storeName, 'readwrite');
      let store = transaction.objectStore(this.storeName);

      let request = store.put(value, key);

      request.onsuccess = event => {
        resolve();
      };

      request.onerror = event => {
        reject(request.error);
      };
    }));
}
```

Now we finally have the `IndexedDBStorage` property that can do a real drop-in replacement for the client that supports the interface. We are also going to add simple permission checking with a plain object that describes the permission of read and write:

```
interface Permission {
  write: boolean;
  read: boolean;
}
```

Then we will add permission checking for method `get` and `set` separately:

```
get<T>(key: string): Promise<T> {
  if (!this.permission.read) {
    return Promise.reject<T>(new Error('Permission denied'));
  }

  // ...
}
```

```
set<T>(key: string, value: T): Promise<void> {
  if (!this.permission.write) {
    return Promise.reject(new Error('Permission denied'));
  }

  // ...
}
```

You may recall Decorator Pattern when you are thinking about the permission checking part, and decorators could be used to simplify the lines written. Try to use decorator syntax to implement this permission checking yourself.

Consequences

The implementation of Proxy Pattern can usually be treated as the encapsulation of the operations to specific objects or targets. It is easy to have the encapsulation augmented without extra burden on the client.

For example, a working online database proxy could do much more than just acting like a plain surrogate. It may cache data and changes locally, or synchronize on schedule without the client being aware.

Summary

In this chapter, we learned about structural design patterns including Composite, Decorator, Adapter, Bridge, Façade, Flyweight, and Proxy. Again we found some of these patterns are highly inter related and even similar to each other to some degree.

For example, we mixed Composite Pattern with Decorator Pattern, Adapter Pattern with Proxy Pattern, compared Adapter Pattern and Bridge Pattern. During the journey of exploring, we sometimes found it was just a natural result to have our code end in a pattern that's similar to what we've listed if we took writing *better code* into consideration.

Taking Adapter Pattern and Bridge Pattern as an example, when we are trying to make two classes cooperate, it comes out with Adapter Pattern and when we are planning on connecting with different classes in advance, it goes with Bridge Pattern. There are no actual lines between each pattern and the applications of those patterns, though the techniques behind patterns could usually be useful.

In the next chapter, we are going to talk about behavioral patterns that help to form algorithms and assign the responsibilities.

5
Behavioral Design Patterns

As the name suggests, behavioral design patterns are patterns about how objects or classes interact with each other. The implementation of behavioral design patterns usually requires certain data structures to support the interaction in a system. However, behavioral patterns and structural patterns focus on different aspects when applied. As a result, you might find patterns in the category of behavioral design patterns usually have simpler or more straightforward structures compared to structural design patterns.

In this chapter, we are going to talk about some of the following common behavioral patterns:

- **Chain of Responsibility**: Organizes behaviors with different scopes
- **Command**: Exposes commands from the internal with encapsulated context
- **Memento**: Provides an approach for managing states outside of their owners without exposing detailed implementations
- **Iterator**: Provides a universal interface for traversing
- **Mediator**: It groups coupling and logically related objects and makes interconnections cleaner in a system that manages many objects

Chain of Responsibility Pattern

There are many scenarios under which we might want to apply certain actions that can fall back from a detailed scope to a more general one.

A nice example would be the help information of a GUI application: when a user requests help information for a certain part of the user interface, it is expected to show information as specific as possible. This can be done with different implementations, and the most intuitive one for a web developer could be events bubbling.

Consider a DOM structure like this:

```
<div class="outer">
  <div class="inner">
    <span class="origin"></span>
  </div>
</div>
```

If a user clicks on the `span.origin` element, a `click` event would start bubbling from the `span` element to the document root (if `useCapture` is `false`):

```
$('.origin').click(event => {
  console.log('Click on `span.origin`.');
});

$('.outer').click(event => {
  console.log('Click on `div.outer`.');
});
```

By default, it will trigger both event listeners added in the preceding code. To stop the propagation as soon as an event gets handled, we can call its `stopPropagation` method:

```
$('.origin').click(event => {
  console.log('Click on `span.origin`.');
  event.stopPropagation();
});

$('.outer').click(event => {
  Console.log('Click on `div.outer`.');
});
```

Though a `click` event is not exactly the same as the help information request, with the support of custom events, it's quite easy to handle help information with necessary detailed or general information in the same chain.

Another important implementation of the Chain of Responsibility Pattern is related to error handling. A primitive example for this could be using `try...catch`. Consider code like this: we have three functions: `foo`, `bar`, and `biu`, `foo` is called by `bar` while `bar` is called by `biu`:

```
function foo() {
  // throw some errors.
}

function bar() {
  foo();
}
```

```
function biu() {
  bar();
}

biu();
```

Inside both functions `bar` and `biu`, we can do some error catching. Assuming function `foo` throws two kinds of errors:

```
function foo() {
  let value = Math.random();

  if (value < 0.5) {
    throw new Error('Awesome error');
  } else if (value < 0.8) {
    throw new TypeError('Awesome type error');
  }
}
```

In function `bar` we would like to handle the `TypeError` and leave other errors throwing on:

```
function bar() {
  try {
    foo();
  } catch (error) {
    if (error instanceof TypeError) {
      console.log('Some type error occurs', error);
    } else {
      throw error;
    }
  }
}
```

And in function `biu`, we would like to add more general handling that catches all the errors so that the program will not crash:

```
function biu() {
  try {
    bar();
  } catch (error) {
    console.log('Some error occurs', error);
  }
}
```

So by using `try...catch` statements, you may have been using the Chain of Responsibility Pattern constantly without paying any attention to it. Just like you may have been using other well-known design patterns all the time.

If we abstract the structure of Chain of Responsibility Pattern into objects, we could have something as illustrated in the figure:

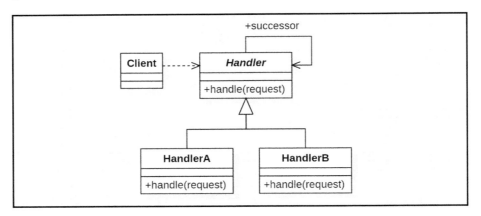

Participants

The participants of the Chain of Responsibility Pattern include:

- **Handler**: Defines the interface of the handler with successor and method to handle requests. This is done implicitly with classes like `EventEmitter` and `try...catch` syntax.
- **Concrete handler**: `EventListener`, `catch` block and `HandlerA`/`HandlerB` in the class version. Defines handlers in the form of callbacks, code blocks and classes that handle requests.
- **Client**: Initiates the requests that go through the chain.

Pattern scope

The Chain of Responsibility Pattern itself could be applied to many different scopes in a program. It requires a multi-level chain to work, but this chain could be in different forms. We've been playing with events as well as `try...catch` statements that have structural levels, this pattern could also be applied to scenarios that have logical levels.

Consider objects marked with different scopes using string:

```
let objectA = {
  scope: 'user.installation.package'
};

let objectB = {
  scope: 'user.installation'
};
```

Now we have two objects with related scopes specified by string, and by adding filters to these scope strings, we can apply operations from specific ones to general ones.

Implementation

In this part, we are going to implement the class version we've mentioned at the end of the introduction to the Chain of Responsibility Pattern. Consider requests that could either ask for help information or feedback prompts:

```
type RequestType = 'help' | 'feedback';

interface Request {
  type: RequestType;
}
```

 We are using string literal type here with union type. It is a pretty useful feature provided in TypeScript that plays well with existing JavaScript coding styles.
See the following link for more information: `http://www.typescriptlang.org/docs/handbook/advanced-types.html`.

One of the key processes for this pattern is going through the handlers' chain and finding out the most specific handler that's available for the request. There are several ways to achieve this: by recursively invoking the `handle` method of a successor, or having a separate logic walking through the handler successor chain until the request is confirmed as handled.

The logic walking through the chain in the second way requires the acknowledgment of whether a request has been properly handled. This can be done either by a state indicator on the request object or by the return value of the `handle` method.

We'll go with the recursive implementation in this part. Firstly, we want the default handling behavior of a handler to be forwarding requests to its successor if any:

```
class Handler {
  private successor: Handler;

  handle(request: Request): void {
    if (this.successor) {
      this.successor.handle(request);
    }
  }
}
```

And now for `HelpHandler`, it handles help requests but forwards others:

```
class HelpHandler extends Handler {
  handle(request: Request): void {
    if (request.type === 'help') {
      // Show help information.
    } else {
      super.handle(request);
    }
  }
}
```

The code for `FeedbackHandler` is similar:

```
class FeedbackHandler extends Handler {
  handle(request: Request): void {
    if (request.type === 'feedback') {
      // Prompt for feedback.
    } else {
      super.handle(request);
    }
  }
}
```

Thus, a chain of handlers could be made up in some way. And if a request got in this chain, it would be passed on until a handler recognizes and handles it. However, it is not necessary to have all requests *handled* after processing them. The handlers can always pass a request on whether this request gets processed by this handler or not.

Consequences

The Chain of Responsibility Pattern decouples the connection between objects that issue the requests and logic that handles those requests. The sender assumes that its requests could, but not necessarily, be properly handled without knowing the details. For some implementations, it is also very easy to add new responsibilities to a specific handler on the chain. This provides notable flexibility for handling requests.

Besides the examples we've been talking about, there is another important mutation of `try...catch` that can be treated in the Chain of Responsibility Pattern – Promise. Within a smaller scope, the chain could be represented as:

```
promise
  .catch(TypeError, reason => {
    // handles TypeError.
  })
  .catch(ReferenceError, reason => {
    // handles ReferenceError.
  })
  .catch(reason => {
    // handles other errors.
  });
```

 The standard `catch` method on an ES Promise object does not provide the overload that accepts an error type as a parameter, but many implementations do.

In a larger scope, this chain would usually appear when the code is playing with third-party libraries. A common usage would be converting errors produced by other libraries to errors known to the current project. We'll talk more about error handling of asynchronous code later in this book.

Command Pattern

Command Pattern involves encapsulating operations as executable commands and could either be in the form of objects or functions in JavaScript. It is common that we may want to make operations rely on certain context and states that are not accessible for the invokers. By storing those pieces of information with a command and passing it out, this situation could be properly handled.

Consider an extremely simple example: we want to provide a function called `wait`, which returns a `cancel` handler:

```
function wait() {
  let $layer = $('.wait-layer');
  $layer.show();
  return () => {
    $layer.hide();
  };
}

let cancel = wait();

setTimeout(() => cancel(), 1000);
```

The `cancel` handler in the preceding code is just a command we were talking about. It stores the context (`$layer`) using closure and is passed out as the return value of function `wait`.

Closure in JavaScript provides a really simple way to store command context and states, however, the direct disadvantage would be compromised flexibility between context/states and command functions because closure is lexically determined and cannot be changed at runtime. This would be okay if the command is only expected to be invoked with fixed context and states, but for more complex situations, we might need to construct them as objects with a proper data structure.

The following diagram shows the overall relations between participants of Command Pattern:

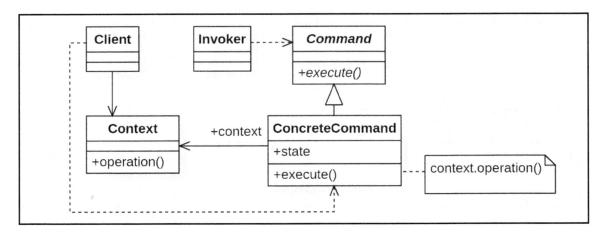

By properly splitting apart context and states with the command object, Command Pattern could also play well with Flyweight Pattern if you wanted to reuse command objects multiple times.

Other common extensions based on Command Pattern include undo support and macros with multiple commands. We are going to play with those later in the implementation part.

Participants

The participants of Command Pattern include:

- **Command**: Defines the general interface of commands passing around, it could be a function signature if the commands are in the form of functions.
- **Concrete command**: Defines the specific behaviors and related data structure. It could also be a function that matches the signature declared as `Command`. The `cancel` handler in the very first example is a concrete command.
- **Context**: The context or receiver that the command is associated with. In the first example, it is the `$layer`.
- **Client**: Creates concrete commands and their contexts.
- **Invoker**: Executes concrete commands.

Pattern scope

Command Pattern suggests two separate parts in a single application or a larger system: *client* and *invoker*. In the simplified example `wait` and `cancel`, it could be hard to distinguish the difference between those parts. But the line is clear: *client* knows or controls the context of commands to be executed with, while *invoker* does not have access or does not need to care about that information.

The key to the Command Pattern is the separation and bridging between those two parts through commands that store context and states.

Implementation

It's common for an editor to expose commands for third-party extensions to modify the text content. Consider a TextContext that contains information about the text file being edited and an abstract TextCommand class associated with that context:

```
class TextContext {
  content = 'text content';
}

abstract class TextCommand {
  constructor(
    public context: TextContext
  ) { }

  abstract execute(...args: any[]): void;
}
```

Certainly, TextContext could contain much more information like language, encoding, and so on. You can add them in your own implementation for more functionality. Now we are going to create two commands: ReplaceCommand and InsertCommand.

```
class ReplaceCommand extends TextCommand {
  execute(index: number, length: number, text: string): void {
    let content = this.context.content;

    this.context.content =
      content.substr(0, index) +
      text +
      content.substr(index + length);
  }
}

class InsertCommand extends TextCommand {
  execute(index: number, text: string): void {
    let content = this.context.content;

    this.context.content =
      content.substr(0, index) +
      text +
      content.substr(index);
  }
}
```

Those two commands share similar logic and actually InsertCommand can be treated as a subset of ReplaceCommand. Or if we have a new delete command, then replace command can be treated as the combination of delete and insert commands.

Now let's assemble those commands with the client and invoker:

```
class Client {
  private context = new TextContext();

  replaceCommand = new ReplaceCommand(this.context);
  insertCommand = new InsertCommand(this.context);
}

let client = new Client();

$('.replace-button').click(() => {
  client.replaceCommand.execute(0, 4, 'the');
});

$('.insert-button').click(() => {
  client.insertCommand.execute(0, 'awesome ');
});
```

If we go further, we can actually have a command that executes other commands. Namely, we can have macro commands. Though the preceding example alone does not make it necessary to create a macro command, there would be scenarios where macro commands help. As those commands are already associated with their contexts, a macro command usually does not need to have an explicit context:

```
interface TextCommandInfo {
  command: TextCommand,
  args: any[];
}

class MacroTextCommand {
  constructor(
    public infos: TextCommandInfo[]
  ) { }

  execute(): void {
    for (let info of this.infos) {
      info.command.execute(...info.args);
    }
  }
}
```

Consequences

Command Pattern decouples the client (who knows or controls context) and the invoker (who has no access to or does not care about detailed context).

It plays well with Composite Pattern. Consider the example of macro commands we mentioned above: a macro command can have other macro commands as its components, thus we make it a composite command.

Another important case of Command Pattern is adding support for undo operations. A direct approach is to add the undo method to every command. When an undo operation is requested, invoke the undo method of commands in reverse order, and we can pray that every command would be undone correctly. However, this approach relies heavily on a flawless implementation of the undo method as every mistake will accumulate. To implement more stable undo support, redundant information or snapshots could be stored.

Memento Pattern

We've talked about an undo support implementation in the previous section on the Command Pattern, and found it was not easy to implement the mechanism purely based on reversing all the operations. However, if we take snapshots of objects as their history, we may manage to avoid accumulating mistakes and make the system more stable. But then we have a problem: we need to store the states of objects while the states are encapsulated with objects themselves.

Memento Pattern helps in this situation. While a memento carries the state of an object at a certain time point, it also controls the process of setting the state back to an object. This makes the internal state implementation hidden from the undo mechanism in the following example:

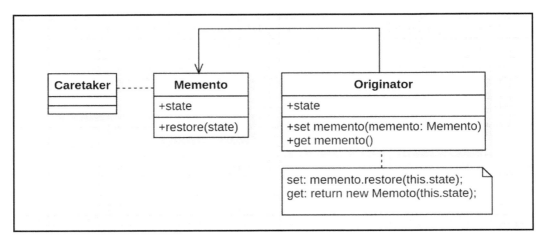

We have the instances of the memento controlling the state restoration in the preceding structure. It can also be controlled by the caretaker, namely the undo mechanism, for simple state restoring cases.

Participants

The participants of Memento Pattern include:

- **Memento**: Stores the state of an object and defines method `restore` or other APIs for restoring the states to specific objects
- **Originator**: Deals with objects that need to have their internal states stored
- **Caretaker**: Manages mementos without intervening with what's inside

Pattern scope

Memento Pattern mainly does two things: it prevents the caretaker from knowing the internal state implementation and decouples the state retrieving and restoring process from states managed by the `Caretaker` or `Originator`.

When the state retrieving and restoring processes are simple, having separated mementos does not help much if you are already keeping the decoupling idea in mind.

Implementation

Start with an empty `State` interface and `Memento` class. As we do not want `Caretaker` to know the details about state inside an `Originator` or `Memento`, we would like to make `state` property of `Memento` private. Having restoration logic inside `Memento` does also help with this, and thus we need method `restore`. So that we don't need to expose a public interface for reading state inside a memento.

And as an object assignment in JavaScript assigns only its reference, we would like to do a quick copy for the states (assuming state objects are single-level):

```
interface State { }

class Memento {
  private state: State;

  constructor(state: State) {
    this.state = Object.assign({} as State, state);
```

```
  }

  restore(state: State): void {
    Object.assign(state, this.state);
  }
}
```

For `Originator` we use a getter and a setter for creating and restoring specific mementos:

```
class Originator {
  state: State;

  get memento(): Memento {
    return new Memento(this.state);
  }

  set memento(memento: Memento) {
    memento.restore(this.state);
  }
}
```

Now the `Caretaker` would manage the history accumulated with mementos:

```
class Caretaker {
  originator: Originator;
  history: Memento[] = [];

  save(): void {
    this.history.push(this.originator.memento);
  }

  restore(): void {
    this.originator.memento = this.history.shift();
  }
}
```

In some implementations of Memento Pattern, a `getState` method is provided for instances of `Originator` to read state from a memento. But to prevent classes other than `Originator` from accessing the `state` property, it may rely on language features like a *friend modifier* to restrict the access (which is not yet available in TypeScript).

Consequences

Memento Pattern makes it easier for a caretaker to manage the states of originators and it becomes possible to extend state retrieving and restoring. However, a perfect implementation that seals everything might rely on language features as we've mentioned before. Using mementos could also bring a performance cost as they usually contain redundant information in trade of stability.

Iterator Pattern

Iterator Pattern provides a universal interface for accessing internal elements of an aggregate without exposing the underlying data structure. A typical iterator contains the following methods or getters:

- `first()`: moves the cursor to the *first* element in the aggregates
- `next()`: moves the cursor to the *next* element
- `end`: a getter that returns a Boolean indicates whether the cursor is at the end
- `item`: a getter that returns the element at the position of the current cursor
- `index`: a getter that returns the index of the element at the current cursor

Iterators for aggregates with different interfaces or underlying structures usually end with different implementations as shown in the following figure:

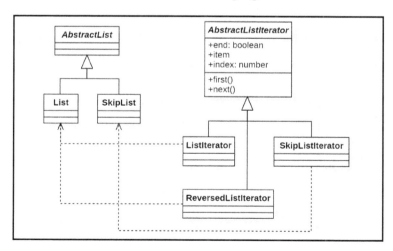

Though the client does not have to worry about the structure of an aggregate, an iterator would certainly need to. Assuming we have everything we need to build an iterator, there could be a variety of ways for creating one. The factory method is widely used when creating iterators, or a *factory getter* if no parameter is required.

Starting with ES6, syntax sugar `for...of` is added and works for all objects with property `Symbol.iterator`. This makes it even easier and more comfortable for developers to work with customized lists and other classes that can be iterated.

Participants

The participants of Iterator Pattern include:

- **Iterator**: `AbstractListIterator`

    Defines the universal iterator interface that is going to transverse different aggregates.

- **Concrete iterator**: `ListIterator`, `SkipListIterator` and `ReversedListIterator`

    Implements specific iterator that transverses and keeps track of a specific aggregate.

- **Aggregate**: `AbstractList`

    Defines a basic interface of aggregates that iterators are going to work with.

- **Concreate aggregate**: `List` and `SkipList`

    Defines the data structure and factory method/getter for creating associated iterators.

Pattern scope

Iterator Pattern provides a unified interface for traversing aggregates. In a system that doesn't rely on iterators, the main functionality provided by iterators could be easily taken over by simple helpers. However, the reusability of those helpers could be reduced as the system grows.

Implementation

In this part, we are going to implement a straightforward array iterator, as well as an ES6 iterator.

Simple array iterator

Let's start by creating an iterator for a JavaScript array, which should be extremely easy. Firstly, the universal interface:

```
interface Iterator<T> {
  first(): void;
  next(): void;
  end: boolean;
  item: T;
  index: number;
}
```

 Please notice that the TypeScript declaration for ES6 has already declared an interface called `Iterator`. Consider putting the code in this part into a namespace or module to avoid conflicts.

And the implementation of a simple array iterator could be:

```
class ArrayIterator<T> implements Iterator<T> {
  index = 0;

  constructor(
    public array: T[]
  ) { }

  first(): void {
    this.index = 0;
  }

  next(): void {
    this.index++;
  }

  get end(): boolean {
    return this.index >= this.array.length;
  }

  get item(): T {
    return this.array[this.index];
```

```
    }
  }
```

Now we need to extend the prototype of native `Array` to add an `iterator` getter:

```
Object.defineProperty(Array.prototype, 'iterator', {
  get() {
    return new ArrayIterator(this);
  }
});
```

To make `iterator` a valid property of the `Array` instance, we also need to extend the interface of `Array`:

```
interface Array<T> {
  iterator: IteratorPattern.Iterator<T>;
}
```

 This should be written outside the namespace under the global scope. Or if you are in a module or ambient module, you might want to try `declare global { ... }` for adding new properties to existing global interfaces.

ES6 iterator

ES6 provides syntax sugar `for...of` and other helpers for *iterable* objects, namely the objects that have implemented the `Iterable` interface of the following:

```
interface IteratorResult<T> {
  done: boolean;
  value: T;
}

interface Iterator<T> {
  next(value?: any): IteratorResult<T>;
  return?(value?: any): IteratorResult<T>;
  throw?(e?: any): IteratorResult<T>;
}

interface Iterable<T> {
  [Symbol.iterator](): Iterator<T>;
}
```

Assume we have a class with the following structure:

```
class SomeData<T> {
  array: T[];
}
```

And we would like to make it iterable. More specifically, we would like to make it iterates reversely. As the `Iterable` interface suggests, we just need to add a method with a special name `Symbol.iterator` for creating an `Iterator`. Let's call the iterator `SomeIterator`:

```
class SomeIterator<T> implements Iterator<T> {
  index: number;

  constructor(
    public array: T[]
  ) {
    this.index = array.length - 1;
  }

  next(): IteratorResult<T> {
    if (this.index <= this.array.length) {
      return {
        value: undefined,
        done: true
      };
    } else {
      return {
        value: this.array[this.index--],
        done: false
      }
    }
  }
}
```

And then define the `iterator` method:

```
class SomeData<T> {
  array: T[];

  [Symbol.iterator]() {
    return new SomeIterator<T>(this.array);
  }
}
```

Now we would have `SomeData` that works with `for...of`.

 Iterators also play well with generators; see the following link for more examples: `https://developer.mozilla.org/en-US/docs/Web/JavaScript/Reference/Iteration_protocols`.

Consequences

Iterator Pattern decouples iteration usage from the data structure that is being iterated. The direct benefit of this is enabling an interchangeable data class that may have completely different internal structures, like an array and binary tree. Also, one data structure can be iterated via different iterators with different traversal mechanisms and results in different orders and efficiencies.

A unified iterator interface in one system could also help the developer from being confused when facing different aggregates. As we mentioned previously, some language like your beloved JavaScript provides a language level abstraction for iterators and makes life even easier.

Mediator Pattern

The connections between UI components and related objects could be extremely complex. Object-oriented programming distributes functionalities among objects. This makes coding easier with cleaner and more intuitive logic; however, it does not ensure the reusability and sometimes makes it difficult to understand if you look at the code again after some days (you may still understand every single operation but would be confused about the interconnections if the network becomes really intricate).

Consider a page for editing user profile. There are standalone inputs like nickname and tagline, as well as inputs that are related to each other. Taking location selection for example, there could easily be a tree-level location and the options available in lower levels are determined by the selection of higher levels. However, if those objects are managed directly by a single huge controller, it will result in a page that has limited reusability. The code formed under this situation would also tend to have a hierarchy that's less clean for people to understand.

Mediator Pattern tries to solve this problem by separating coupling elements and objects as groups, and adding a *director* between a group of elements and other objects as shown in the following figure:

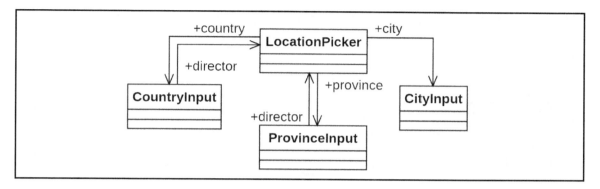

Those objects form a mediator with their colleagues that can interact with other objects as a single object. With proper encapsulation, the mediator will have better reusability as it has just the right size and properly divided functionality. In the world of web front end development, there are concepts or implementations that fit Mediator Pattern well, like *Web Component* and *React*.

Participants

The participants of Mediator Pattern include:

- **Mediator**:

  Usually, the abstraction or skeleton predefined by a framework. Defines the interface that colleagues in a mediator communicate through.

- **Concrete mediator**: LocationPicker

  Manages the colleagues and makes them cooperate, providing a higher level interface for objects outside.

- **Colleague classes**: CountryInput, ProvinceInput, CityInput

  Defines references to their mediator and notifies its changes to the mediator and accepts modifications issued by the mediator.

Pattern scope

Mediator Pattern could connect many parts of a project, but does not have direct or enormous impact on the outline. Most of the credit is given because of increased usability and cleaner interconnections introduced by mediators. However, along with a nice overall architecture, Mediator Pattern can help a lot with refined code quality, and make the project easier to maintain.

Implementation

Using libraries like React would make it very easy to implement Mediator Pattern, but for now, we are going with a relatively primitive way and handle changes by hand. Let's think about the result we want for a `LocationPicker` we've discussed, and hopefully, it includes `country`, `province` and `city` fields:

```
interface LocationResult {
  country: string;
  province: string;
  city: string;
}
```

And now we can sketch the overall structure of class `LocationPicker`:

```
class LocationPicker {
  $country = $(document.createElement('select'));
  $province = $(document.createElement('select'));
  $city = $(document.createElement('select'));

  $element = $(document.createElement('div'))
    .append(this.$country)
    .append(this.$province)
    .append(this.$city);

  get value(): LocationResult {
    return {
      country: this.$country.val(),
      province: this.$province.val(),
      city: this.$city.val()
    };
  }
}
```

Before we can tell how the colleagues are going to cooperate, we would like to add a helper method `setOptions` for updating options in a `select` element:

```
private static setOptions(
  $select: JQuery,
  values: string[]
): void {
  $select.empty();

  let $options = values.map(value => {
    return $(document.createElement('option'))
      .text(value)
      .val(value);
  });

  $select.append($options);
}
```

I personally tend to have methods that do not depend on a specific instance static methods and this applies to methods `getCountries`, `getProvincesByCountry`, and `getCitiesByCountryAndProvince` that simply return a list by the information given as function arguments (though we are not going to actually implement that part):

```
private static getCountries(): string[] {
  return ['-'].concat([/* countries */]);
}

private static getProvincesByCountry(country: string): string[] {
  return ['-'].concat([/* provinces */]);
}

private static getCitiesByCountryAndProvince(
  country: string,
  province: string
): string[] {
  return ['-'].concat([/* cities */]);
}
```

Now we may add methods for updating options in the `select` elements:

```
updateProvinceOptions(): void {
  let country: string = this.$country.val();

  let provinces = LocationPicker.getProvincesByCountry(country);
  LocationPicker.setOptions(this.$province, provinces);

  this.$city.val('-');
```

```
  }

  updateCityOptions(): void {
    let country: string = this.$country.val();
    let province: string = this.$province.val();

    let cities = LocationPicker
      .getCitiesByCountryAndProvince(country, province);
    LocationPicker.setOptions(this.$city, cities);
  }
```

Finally, weave those colleagues together and add listeners to the change events:

```
constructor() {
  LocationPicker
    .setOptions(this.$country, LocationPicker.getCountries());
  LocationPicker.setOptions(this.$province, ['-']);
  LocationPicker.setOptions(this.$city, ['-']);

  this.$country.change(() => {
    this.updateProvinceOptions();
  });

  this.$province.change(() => {
    this.updateCityOptions();
  });
}
```

Consequences

Mediator Pattern, like many other design patterns, downgrades a level-100 problem into two level-10 problems and solves them separately. A well-designed mediator usually has a proper size and usually tends to be reused in the future. For example, we might not want to put nickname input together with the country, province, and city inputs as this combination doesn't tend to occur in other situations (which means they are not strongly related).

As the project evolves, a mediator may grow to a size that's not efficient anymore. So a properly designed mediator should also take the dimension of time into consideration.

Summary

In this chapter, we talked about some common behavioral patterns for different scopes and different scenarios. Chain of Responsibility Pattern and Command Pattern can apply to a relatively wide range of scopes, while other patterns mentioned in this chapter usually care more about the scope with objects and classes directly related.

Behavioral patterns we've talked about in this chapter are less like each other compared to creational patterns and structural patterns we previously walked through. Some of the behavioral patterns could compete with others, but many of them could cooperate. For example, we talked about Command Pattern with Memento Pattern to implement undo support. Many others may cooperate in parallel and do their own part.

In the next chapter, we'll continue talking about other behavioral design patterns that are useful and widely used.

6
Behavioral Design Patterns: Continuous

In the previous chapter, we've already talked about some of the behavioral design patterns. We'll be continuing with more patterns in this category in this chapter, including: Strategy Pattern, State Pattern, Template Method Pattern, Observer Pattern, and Visitor Pattern.

Many of these patterns share the same idea: unify the shape and vary the details. Here is a quick overview:

- **Strategy Pattern** and **Template Pattern**: Defines the same outline of algorithms
- **State Pattern**: Provides different behavior for objects in different states with the same interface
- **Observer Pattern**: Provides a unified process of handling subject changes and notifying observers
- **Visitor Pattern**: Does similar jobs as Strategy Pattern sometimes, but avoids an over complex interface that might be required for Strategy Pattern to handle objects in many different types

Patterns that will be discussed in this chapter could be applied in different scopes just as many patterns in other categories.

Strategy Pattern

It's common that a program has similar outlines for processing different targets with different detailed algorithms. Strategy Pattern encapsulates those algorithms and makes them interchangeable within the shared outline.

Consider conflicting merging processes of data synchronization, which we talked about in Chapter 2, *The Challenge of Increasing Complexity*. Before refactoring, the code was like this:

```
if (type === 'value') {
  // ...
} else if (type === 'increment') {
  // ...
} else if (type === 'set') {
  // ...
}
```

But later we found out that we could actually extract the same outlines from different phases of the synchronization process, and encapsulate them as different strategies. After refactoring, the outline of the code became as follows:

```
let strategy = strategies[type];
strategy.operation();
```

We get a lot of ways to compose and organize those strategy objects or classes sometimes in JavaScript. A possible structure for Strategy Pattern could be:

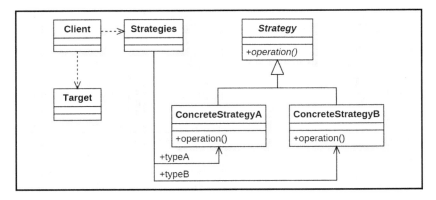

In this structure, the client is responsible for fetching specific strategies from the table and applying operations of the current phase.

Another structure is using contextual objects and letting them control their own strategies:

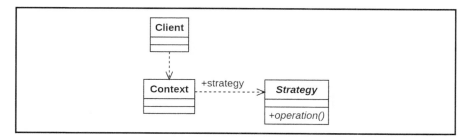

Thus the client needs only to link a specific context with the corresponding strategy.

Participants

We've mentioned two possible structures for Strategy Pattern, so let's discuss the participants separately. For the first structure, the participants include the following:

- **Strategy**

    Defines the interface of strategy objects or classes.

- **Concrete strategy**: ConcreteStrategyA and ConcreteStrategyB

    Implements concrete strategy operations defined by the Strategy interface.

- **Strategy manager**: Strategies

    Defines a data structure to manage strategy objects. In the example, it's just a simple hash table that uses data type names as keys and strategy objects as values. It could be more complex on demand: for example, with matching patterns or conditions.

- **Target**

    The target to apply algorithms defined in strategy objects.

- **Client**

    Makes targets and strategies cooperate.

The participants of the second structure include the following:

- **Strategy** and **concrete strategy**

  The same as in the preceding section.

- **Context**

  Defines a reference to the strategy object applied. Provides related methods or property getters for clients to operate.

- **Client**

  Manages context objects.

Pattern scope

Strategy Pattern is usually applied to scopes with small or medium sizes. It provides a way to encapsulate algorithms and makes those algorithms easier to manage under the same outline. Strategy Pattern can also be the core of an entire solution sometimes, and a good example is the synchronization implementation we've been playing with. In this case, Strategy Pattern builds the bridge of plugins and makes the system extendable. But most of the time, the fundamental work done by Strategy Pattern is decoupling concrete strategies, contexts, or targets.

Implementation

The implementation starts with defining the interfaces of objects we'll be playing with. We have two target types in string literal type `'a'` and `'b'`. Targets of type `'a'` have a `result` property with type `string`, while targets of type `'b'` have a `value` property with type `number`.

The interfaces we'll have look, are like:

```
type TargetType = 'a' | 'b';

interface Target {
  type: TargetType;
}

interface TargetA extends Target {
  type: 'a';
```

```
    result: string;
}

interface TargetB extends Target {
  type: 'b';
  value: number;
}

interface Strategy<TTarget extends Target> {
  operationX(target: TTarget): void;
  operationY(target: TTarget): void;
}
```

Now we'll define the concrete strategy objects without a constructor:

```
let strategyA: Strategy<TargetA> = {
  operationX(target) {
    target.result = target.result + target.result;
  },
  operationY(target) {
    target.result = target
      .result
      .substr(Math.floor(target.result.length / 2));
  }
};

let strategyB: Strategy<TargetB> = {
  operationX(target) {
    target.value = target.value * 2;
  },
  operationY(target) {
    target.value = Math.floor(target.value / 2);
  }
};
```

To make it easier for a client to fetch those strategies, we'll put them into a hash table:

```
let strategies: {
  [type: string]: Strategy<Target>
} = {
  a: strategyA,
  b: strategyB
};
```

And now we can make them work with targets in different types:

```
let targets: Target[] = [
  { type: 'a' },
  { type: 'a' },
  { type: 'b' }
];

for (let target of targets) {
  let strategy = strategies[target.type];

  strategy.operationX(target);
  strategy.operationY(target);
}
```

Consequences

Strategy Pattern makes the foreseeable addition of algorithms for contexts or targets under new categories easier. It also makes the outline of a process even cleaner by hiding trivial branches of behaviors selection.

However, the abstraction of algorithms defined by the `Strategy` interface may keep growing while we are trying to add more strategies and satisfy their requirements of parameters. This could be a problem for a Strategy Pattern with clients that are managing targets and strategies. But for the other structures which the references of strategy objects are stored by contexts themselves, we can manage to trade-off the interchangeability. This would result in Visitor Pattern, which we are going to talk about later in this chapter.

And as we've mentioned before, Strategy Pattern can also provide notable extensibility if an extendable strategy manager is available or the client of contexts is designed to.

State Pattern

It's possible for some objects to behave completely differently when they are in different states. Let's think about an easy example first. Consider rendering and interacting with a custom button in two states: enabled and disabled. When the button is enabled, it lights up and changes its style to active on a mouse hover, and of course, it handles clicks; when disabled, it dims and no longer cares about mouse events.

We may think of an abstraction with two operations: `render` (with a parameter that indicates whether the mouse is hovering) and `click`; along with two states: *enabled* and *disabled*. We can even divide deeper and have state *active*, but that won't be necessary in our case.

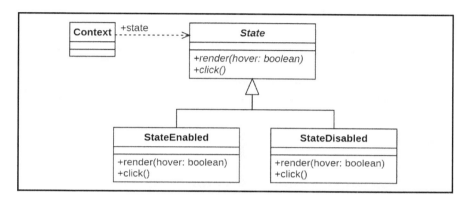

And now we can have `StateEnabled` with both `render` and `click` methods implemented, while having `StateDisabled` with only `render` method implemented because it does not care about the `hover` parameter. In this example, we are expecting every method of the states being callable. So we can have the abstract class `State` with empty `render` and `click` methods.

Participants

The participants of State Pattern include the following:

- **State**

    Defines the interface of state objects that are being switched to internally.

- **Concrete state**: `StateEnabled` and `StateDisabled`

    Implements the `State` interface with behavior corresponding to a specific state of the context. May have an optional reference back to its context.

- **Context**

    Manages references to different states, and makes operations defined on the active one.

Pattern scope

State Pattern usually applies to the code of scopes with the size of a feature. It does not specify whom to transfer the state of context: it could be either the context itself, the state methods, or code that controls context.

Implementation

Start with the `State` interface (it could also be an abstract class if there are operations or logic to share):

```
interface State {
  render(hover: boolean): void;
  click(): void;
}
```

With the `State` interface defined, we can move to `Context` and sketch its outline:

```
class Context {
  $element: JQuery;

  state: State;

  private render(hover: boolean): void {
    this.state.render(hover);
  }

  private click(): void {
    this.state.click();
  }
  onclick(): void {
    console.log('I am clicked.');
  }
}
```

Now we are going to have the two states, `StateEnabled` and `StateDisabled` implemented. First, let's address `StateEnabled`, it cares about `hover` status and handles `click` event:

```
class StateEnabled implements State {
  constructor(
    public context: Context
  ) { }

  render(hover: boolean): void {
```

```
    this
      .context
      .$element
      .removeClass('disabled')
      .toggleClass('hover', hover);
  }

  click(): void {
    this.context.onclick();
  }
}
```

Next, for `StateDisabled` it just ignores `hover` parameter and does nothing when `click` event emits:

```
class StateDisabled implements State {
  constructor(
    public context: Context
  ) { }

  render(): void {
    this
      .context
      .$element
      .addClass('disabled')
      .removeClass('hover');
  }

  click(): void {
    // Do nothing.
  }
}
```

Now we have classes of states *enabled* and *disabled* ready. As the instances of those classes are associated with the context, we need to initialize every state when a new `Context` is initiated:

```
class Context {
  ...

  private stateEnabled = new StateEnabled(this);
  private stateDisabled = new StateDisabled(this);

  state: State = this.stateEnabled;
  ...
}
```

It is possible to use flyweights by passing context in when invoking every operation on the active state as well.

Now let's finish the `Context` by listening to and forwarding proper events:

```
constructor() {
  this
    .$element
    .hover(
      () => this.render(true),
      () => this.render(false)
    )
    .click(() => this.click());

  this.render(false);
}
```

Consequences

State Pattern reduces conditional branches in potentially multiple methods of context objects. As a trade-off, extra state objects are introduced, though it usually won't be a big problem.

The context object in State Pattern usually delegates operations and forwards them to the current state object. Thus operations defined by a concrete state may have access to the context itself. This makes reusing state objects possible with flyweights.

Template Method Pattern

When we are talking about subclassing or inheriting, the building is usually built from the bottom up. Subclasses inherit the basis and then provide more. However, it could be useful to reverse the structure sometimes as well.

Consider Strategy Pattern which defines the outline of a process and has interchangeable algorithms as strategies. If we apply this structure under the hierarchy of classes, we will have Template Method Pattern.

A template method is an abstract method (optionally with default implementation) and acts as a placeholder under the outline of a larger process. Subclasses override or implement related methods to modify or complete the behaviors. Imaging the skeleton of a `TextReader`, we are expecting its subclasses to handle text files from different storage media, detect different encodings and read all the text. We may consider a structure like this:

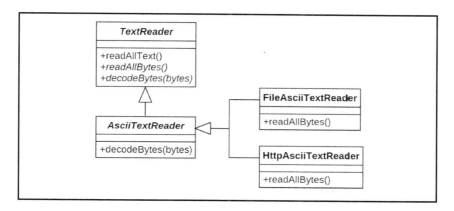

The `TextReader` in this example has a method `readAllText` that reads all text from a resource by two steps: reading all bytes from the resource (`readAllBytes`), and then decoding those bytes with certain encoding (`decodeBytes`).

The structure also suggests the possibility of sharing implementations among concrete classes that implement template methods. We may create an abstract class `AsciiTextReader` that extends `TextReader` and implements method `decodeBytes`. And build concrete classes `FileAsciiTextReader` and `HttpAsciiTextReader` that extend `AsciiTextReader` and implement method `readAllBytes` to handle resources on different storage media.

Participants

The participants of Template Method Pattern include the following:

- **Abstract class**: `TextReader`

    Defines the signatures of template methods, as well as the outline of algorithms that weave everything together.

- **Concrete classes**: `AsciiTextReader`, `FileAsciiTextReader` and `HttpAsciiTextReader`

    Implements template methods defined in abstract classes. Typical concrete classes are `FileAsciiTextReader` and `HttpAsciiTextReader` in this example. However, compared to being abstract, *defining the outline of algorithms* weighs more in the categorization.

Pattern scope

Template Method Pattern is usually applied in a relatively small scope. It provides an extendable way to implement features and avoid redundancy from the upper structure of a series of algorithms.

Implementation

There are two levels of the inheriting hierarchy: the `AsciiTextReader` will subclass `TextReader` as another abstract class. It implements method `decodeBytes` but leaves `readAllBytes` to its subclasses. Starting with the `TextReader`:

```
abstract class TextReader {
  async readAllText(): Promise<string> {
    let bytes = await this.readAllBytes();
    let text = this.decodeBytes(bytes);

    return text;
  }

  abstract async readAllBytes(): Promise<Buffer>;

  abstract decodeBytes(bytes: Buffer): string;
}
```

We are using Promises with `async` and `await` which are coming to ECMAScript next. Please refer to the following links for more information:
https://github.com/Microsoft/TypeScript/issues/1664
https://tc39.github.io/ecmascript-asyncawait/

And now let's subclass `TextReader` as `AsciiTextReader` which still remains abstract:

```
abstract class AsciiTextReader extends TextReader {
  decodeBytes(bytes: Buffer): string {
    return bytes.toString('ascii');
  }
}
```

For `FileAsciiTextReader`, we'll need to import filesystem (`fs`) module of Node.js to perform file reading:

```
import * as FS from 'fs';

class FileAsciiTextReader extends AsciiTextReader {
  constructor(
    public path: string
  ) {
    super();
  }

  async readAllBytes(): Promise<Buffer> {
    return new Promise<Buffer>((resolve, reject) => {
      FS.readFile(this.path, (error, bytes) => {
        if (error) {
          reject(error);
        } else {
          resolve(bytes);
        }
      });
    });
  }
}
```

For `HttpAsciiTextReader`, we are going to use a popular package `request` to send HTTP requests:

```
import * as request from 'request';

class HttpAsciiTextReader extends AsciiTextReader {
  constructor(
    public url: string
  ) {
    super();
  }

  async readAllBytes(): Promise<Buffer> {
    return new Promise<Buffer>((resolve, reject) => {
      request(this.url, {
```

```
      encoding: null
    }, (error, bytes, body) => {
      if (error) {
        reject(error);
      } else {
        resolve(body);
      }
    });
  });
 }
}
```

 Both concrete reader implementations pass resolver functions to the Promise constructor for converting asynchronous Node.js style callbacks to Promises. For more information, read more about the Promise constructor : https://developer.mozilla.org/en-US/docs/Web/JavaSc ript/Reference/Global_Objects/Promise.

Consequences

Compared to Strategy Pattern, Template Method Pattern provides convenience for building objects with the same outline of algorithms outside of the existing system. This makes Template Method Pattern a useful way to build tooling classes instead of fixed processes built-in.

But Template Method Pattern has less runtime flexibility as it does not have a *manager*. It also relies on the client who's using those objects to do the work. And as the implementation of Template Method Pattern relies on subclassing, it could easily result in hierarchies that have a similar code on different branches. Though this could be optimized by using techniques like *mixin*.

Observer Pattern

Observer Pattern is an important Pattern backed by an important idea in software engineering. And it is usually a key part of MVC architecture and its variants as well.

If you have ever written an application with a rich user interface without a framework like Angular or a solution with React, you might probably have struggled with changing class names and other properties of UI elements. More specifically, the code that controls those properties of the same group of elements lies every branch related to the elements in related event listeners, just to keep the elements being correctly updated.

Consider a "Do" button of which the `disabled` property should be determined by the status of a `WebSocket` connection to a server and whether the currently active item is done. Every time the status of either the connection or the active item gets updated, we'll need to update the button correspondingly. The most "handy" way could be two somewhat identical groups of code being put in two event listeners. But in this way, the amount of similar code would just keep growing as more relevant objects get involved.

The problem in this "Do" button example is that, the behavior of code that's controlling the button is driven by primitive events. The heavy load of managing the connections and behaviors among different events is directly taken by the developer who's writing that code. And unfortunately, the complexity in this case, grows exponentially, which means it could easily exceed our brain capacity. Writing code this way might result in more bugs and make maintaining much likely to introduce new bugs.

But the beautiful thing is, we can find the factors that multiply and output the desired result, and the reference for dividing those factors are groups of related states. Still speaking of the "Do" button example, what the button cares about is: connection status and the active item status (assuming they are booleans `connected` and `loaded`). We can have the code written as two parts: one part that changes those states, and another part that updates the button:

```
let button = document.getElementById('do-button');

let connected = false;
let loaded = false;

function updateButton() {
  let disabled = !connected && !loaded;
  button.disabled = disabled;
}

connection.on('statuschange', event => {
  connected = event.connected;
  updateButton();
});

activeItem.on('statuschange', event => {
  loaded = event.loaded;
  updateButton();
});
```

The preceding sample code already has the embryo of Observer Pattern: the subjects (states `connected` and `loaded`) and the observer (`updateButton` function), though we still need to call `updateButton` manually every time any related state changes. An improved structure could look like the following figure:

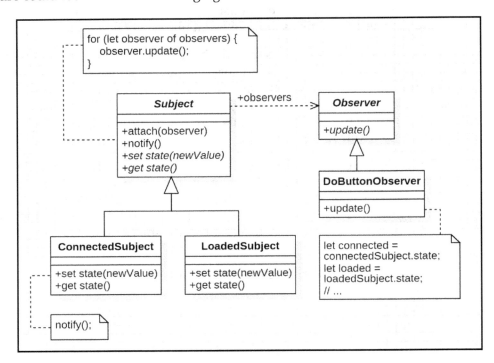

But just like the example we've been talking about, observers in many situations care about more than one state. It could be less satisfying to have subjects attach observers separately.

A solution to this could be multi-state subjects, to achieve that, we can form a composite subject that contains sub-subjects. If a subject receives a `notify` call, it wakes up its observers and at the same time notifies its parent. Thus the observer can attach one composite subject for notifications of changes that happen to multiple states.

However, the process of creating the composite itself could still be annoying. In dynamic programming languages like JavaScript, we may have a state manager that contains specific states handling notifications and attaching observers directly with implicit creations of subjects:

```
let stateManager = new StateManager({
  connected: false,
  loaded: false,
  foo: 'abc',
  bar: 123
});

stateManager.on(['connected', 'loaded'], () => {
  let disabled =
    !stateManager.connected && !stateManager.loaded;
  button.disabled = disabled;
});
```

 In many MV* frameworks, the states to be observed are analyzed automatically from related expressions by built-in parsers or similar mechanisms.

And now the structure gets even simpler:

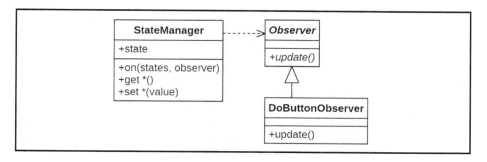

Participants

We've talked about the basic structure of Observer Pattern with subjects and observers, and a variant with implicit subjects. The participants of the basic structure include the following:

- **Subject**

    Subject to be observed. Defines methods to `attach` or `notify` observers. A subject could also be a composite that contains sub-subjects, which allows multiple states to be observed with the same interface.

- **Concrete subject**: `ConnectedSubject` and `LoadedSubject`

    Contains state related to the subject, and implements methods or properties to get and set their state.

- **Observer**

    Defines the interface of an object that reacts when an observation notifies. In JavaScript, it could also be an interface (or signature) of a function.

- **Concrete observer**: `DoButtonObserver`

    Defines the action that reacts to the notifications of subjects being observed. Could be a callback function that matches the signature defined.

In the variant version, the participants include the following:

- **State manager**

    Manages a complex, possibly multi-level state object containing multiple states. Defines the interface to attach observers with subjects, and notifies those observers when a subject changes.

- **Concrete subject**

    Keys to specific states. For example, string `"connected"` may represent state `stateManager.connected`, while string `"foo.bar"` may represent state `stateManager.foo.bar`.

Observer and *concrete observer* are basically the same as described in the former structure. But observers are now notified by the state manager instead of subject objects.

Pattern scope

Observer Pattern is a pattern that may easily structure half of the project. In MV* architectures, Observer Pattern can decouple the view from business logic. The concept of view can be applied to other scenarios related to displaying information as well.

Implementation

Both of the structures we've mentioned should not be hard to implement, though more details should be put into consideration for production code. We'll go with the second implementation that has a central state manager.

 To simplify the implementation, we will use `get` and `set` methods to access specific states by their keys. But many frameworks available might handle those through getters and setters, or other mechanisms.

 To learn about how frameworks like Angular handle states changing, please read their documentation or source code if necessary.

We are going to have `StateManager` inherit `EventEmitter`, so we don't need to care much about issues like multiple listeners. But as we are accepting multiple state keys as subjects, an overload to method `on` will be added. Thus the outline of `StateManager` would be as follows:

```
type Observer = () => void;

class StateManager extends EventEmitter{
  constructor(
    private state: any
  ) {
    super();
  }

  set(key: string, value: any): void { }

  get(key: string): any { }

  on(state: string, listener: Observer): this;
  on(states: string[], listener: Observer): this;
  on(states: string | string[], listener: Observer): this { }
}
```

You might have noticed that method `on` has the return type `this`, which may keep referring to the type of current instance. Type `this` is very helpful for chaining methods.

The keys will be `"foo"` and `"foo.bar"`, we need to split a key as separate identifiers for accessing the value from the `state` object. Let's have a private `_get` method that takes an array of `identifiers` as input:

```
private _get(identifiers: string[]): any {
  let node = this.state;

  for (let identifier of identifiers) {
    node = node[identifier];
  }

  return node;
}
```

Now we can implement method `get` upon `_get`:

```
get(key: string): any {
  let identifiers = key.split('.');
  return this._get(identifiers);
}
```

For method `set`, we can get the parent object of the last identifier of property to be set, so things work like this:

```
set(key: string, value: any): void {
  let identifiers = key.split('.');
  let lastIndex = identifiers.length - 1;

  let node = this._get(identifiers.slice(0, lastIndex));
  node[identifiers[lastIndex]] = value;
}
```

But there's one more thing, we need to notify observers that are observing a certain subject:

```
set(key: string, value: any): void {
  let identifiers = key.split('.');
  let lastIndex = identifiers.length - 1;

  let node = this._get(identifiers.slice(0, lastIndex));
  node[identifiers[lastIndex]] = value;

  for (let i = identifiers.length; i > 0; i--) {
```

```
    let key = identifiers.slice(0, i).join('.');
    this.emit(key);
  }
}
```

When we're done with the notifying part, let's add an overload for method on to support multiple keys:

```
on(state: string, listener: Observer): this;
on(states: string[], listener: Observer): this;
on(states: string | string[], listener: Observer): this {
  if (typeof states === 'string') {
    super.on(states, listener);
  } else {
    for (let state of states) {
      super.on(state, listener);
    }
  }

  return this;
}
```

Problem solved. Now we have a state manager that will work for simple scenarios.

Consequences

Observer Pattern decouples subjects with observers. While an observer may be observing multiple states in subjects at the same time, it usually does not care about which state triggers the notification. As a result, the observer may make *unnecessary* updates that actually do nothing to – for example – the view.

However, the impact on performance could be negligible most of the time, not even need to mention the benefits it brings.

By splitting view and logic apart, Observer Pattern may reduce possible branches significantly. This will help eliminate bugs caused at the coupling part between view and logic. Thus, by properly applying Observer Pattern, the project will be made much more robust and easier to maintain.

However, there are some details we still need care about:

1. The observer that updates the state could cause circular invocation.
2. For more complex data structures like collections, it might be expensive to re-render everything. Observers in this scenario may need more information about the change to only perform necessary updates. View implementations like React do this in another way; they introduce a concept called **Virtual DOM**. By updating and diffing the virtual DOM before re-rendering the actual DOM (which could usually be the bottleneck of performance), it provides a relatively general solution for different data structures.

Visitor Pattern

Visitor Pattern provides a uniformed interface for *visiting* different data or objects while allowing detailed operations in concrete visitors to vary. Visitor Pattern is usually used with composites, and it is widely used for walking through data structures like **abstract syntax tree (AST)**. But to make it easier for those who are not familiar with compiler stuff, we will provide a simpler example.

Consider a DOM-like tree containing multiple elements to render:

```
[
  Text {
    content: "Hello, "
  },
  BoldText {
    content: "TypeScript"
  },
  Text {
    content: "! Popular editors:\n"
  },
  UnorderedList {
    items: [
      ListItem {
        content: "Visual Studio Code"
      },
      ListItem {
        content: "Visual Studio"
      },
      ListItem {
        content: "WebStorm"
      }
    ]
  }
```

```
]
```

The rendering result in HTML would look like this:

```
Hello, <b>TypeScript</b>! Popular editors:
<ul>
<li>Visual Studio Code</li>
<li>Visual Studio</li>
<li>WebStorm</li>
</ul>
```

While in Markdown, it would look like this:

```
Hello, **TypeScript**! Popular editors:

- Visual Studio Code
- Visual Studio
- WebStorm
```

Visitor Pattern allows operations in the same category to be coded in the same place. We'll have concrete visitors, `HTMLVisitor` and `MarkdownVisitor` that take the responsibilities of transforming different nodes by visiting them respectively and recursively. The nodes being visited have a method `accept` for accepting a visitor to perform the transformation. An overall structure of Visitor Pattern could be split into two parts, the first part is the visitor abstraction and its concrete subclasses:

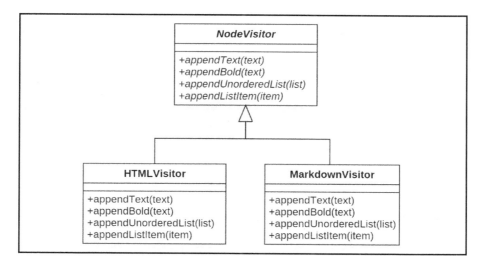

The second part is the abstraction and concrete subclasses of nodes to be visited:

Participants

The participants of Visitor Pattern include the following:

- **Visitor**: `NodeVisitor`

  Defines the interface of operations corresponding to each element class. In languages with static types and method overloading, the method names can be unified. But as it takes extra runtime checking in JavaScript, we'll use different method names to distinguish them. The operation methods are usually named after `visit`, but here we use `append` as its more related to the context.

- **Concrete visitor**: `HTMLVisitor` and `MarkdownVisitor`

  Implements every operation of the concrete visitor, and handles internal states if any.

- **Element**: `Node`

  Defines the interface of the element accepting the visitor instance. The method is usually named `accept`, though here we are using `appendTo` for a better matching with the context. Elements could themselves be composites and pass visitors on with their child elements.

- **Concrete element**: `Text, BoldText, UnorderedList` and `ListItem`

  Implements `accept` method and calls the method from the visitor instance corresponding to the element instance itself.

- **Client**:

  Enumerates elements and applies visitors to them.

Pattern scope

Visitor Pattern can form a large feature inside a system. For some programs under certain categories, it may also form the core architecture. For example, *Babel* uses Visitor Pattern for AST transforming and a plugin for Babel is actually a visitor that can visit and transform elements it cares about.

Implementation

We are going to implement `HTMLVisitor` and `MarkdownVisitor` which may transform nodes to text, as we've talked about. Start with the upper abstraction:

```
interface Node {
  appendTo(visitor: NodeVisitor): void;
}

interface NodeVisitor {
  appendText(text: Text): void;
  appendBold(text: BoldText): void;
  appendUnorderedList(list: UnorderedList): void;
  appendListItem(item: ListItem): void;
}
```

Continue with concrete nodes that do similar things, `Text` and `BoldText`:

```
class Text implements Node {
  constructor(
    public content: string
  ) { }

  appendTo(visitor: NodeVisitor): void {
    visitor.appendText(this);
  }
}
```

```
class BoldText implements Node {
  constructor(
    public content: string
  ) { }

  appendTo(visitor: NodeVisitor): void {
    visitor.appendBold(this);
  }
}
```

And list stuff:

```
class UnorderedList implements Node {
  constructor(
    public items: ListItem[]
  ) { }

  appendTo(visitor: NodeVisitor): void {
    visitor.appendUnorderedList(this);
  }
}

class ListItem implements Node {
  constructor(
    public content: string
  ) { }

  appendTo(visitor: NodeVisitor): void {
    visitor.appendListItem(this);
  }
}
```

Now we have the elements of a structure to be visited, we'll begin to implement concrete visitors. Those visitors will have an `output` property for the transformed string. `HTMLVisitor` goes first:

```
class HTMLVisitor implements NodeVisitor {
  output = '';

  appendText(text: Text) {
    this.output += text.content;
  }

  appendBold(text: BoldText) {
    this.output += `<b>${text.content}</b>`;
  }

  appendUnorderedList(list: UnorderedList) {
```

```
    this.output += '<ul>';

    for (let item of list.items) {
      item.appendTo(this);
    }

    this.output += '</ul>';
  }

  appendListItem(item: ListItem) {
    this.output += `<li>${item.content}</li>`;
  }
}
```

Pay attention to the loop inside `appendUnorderedList`, it handles visiting of its own list items.

A similar structure applies to `MarkdownVisitor`:

```
class MarkdownVisitor implements NodeVisitor {
  output = '';

  appendText(text: Text) {
    this.output += text.content;
  }

  appendBold(text: BoldText) {
    this.output += `**${text.content}**`;
  }

  appendUnorderedList(list: UnorderedList) {
    this.output += '\n';

    for (let item of list.items) {
      item.appendTo(this);
    }
  }

  appendListItem(item: ListItem) {
    this.output += `- ${item.content}\n`;
  }
}
```

Now the infrastructures are ready, let's create the tree-like structure we've been imagining since the beginning:

```
let nodes = [
  new Text('Hello, '),
```

```
    new BoldText('TypeScript'),
    new Text('! Popular editors:\n'),
    new UnorderedList([
      new ListItem('Visual Studio Code'),
      new ListItem('Visual Studio'),
      new ListItem('WebStorm')
    ])
];
```

And finally, build the outputs with visitors:

```
let htmlVisitor = new HTMLVisitor();
let markdownVisitor = new MarkdownVisitor();

for (let node of nodes) {
  node.appendTo(htmlVisitor);
  node.appendTo(markdownVisitor);
}

console.log(htmlVisitor.output);
console.log(markdownVisitor.output);
```

Consequences

Both Strategy Pattern and Visitor Pattern could be applied to scenarios of processing objects. But Strategy Pattern relies on clients to handle all related arguments and contexts, this makes it hard to come out with an exquisite abstraction if the expected behaviors of different objects differ a lot. Visitor Pattern solves this problem by decoupling visit actions and operations to be performed.

By passing different visitors, Visitor Pattern can apply different operations to objects without changing other code although it usually means adding new elements and would result in adding related operations to an abstract visitor and all of its concrete subclasses.

Visitors like the NodeVisitor in the previous example may store state itself (in that example, we stored the output of transformed nodes) and more advanced operations can be applied based on the state accumulated. For example, it's possible to determine what has been appended to the output, and thus we can apply different behaviors with the node currently being visited.

However, to complete certain operations, extra public methods may need to be exposed from the elements.

Summary

In this chapter, we've talked about other behavior design patterns as complements to the former chapter, including Strategy, State, Template Method, Observer and Visitor Pattern.

Strategy Pattern is so common and useful that it may appear in a project several times, with different forms. And you might not know you were using Observer Pattern with implementation in a daily framework.

After walking through those patterns, you might find there are many ideas in common behind each pattern. It is worth thinking what's behind them and even letting the outline go in your mind.

In the next chapter, we'll continue with some handy patterns related to JavaScript and TypeScript, and important scenarios of those languages.

7
Patterns and Architectures in JavaScript and TypeScript

In the previous four chapters, we've walked through common and classical design patterns and discussed some of their variants in JavaScript or TypeScript. In this chapter, we'll continue with some architecture and patterns closely related to the language and their common applications. We don't have many pages to expand and certainly cannot cover everything in a single chapter, so please take it as an appetizer and feel free to explore more.

Many topics in this chapter are related to asynchronous programming. We'll start with a web architecture for Node.js that's based on Promise. This is a larger topic that has interesting ideas involved, including abstractions of responses and permissions, as well as error handling tips. Then we'll talk about how to organize modules with **ECMAScript** (**ES**) module syntax. And this chapter will end with several useful asynchronous techniques.

Overall, we'll have the following topics covered in this chapter:

- Architecture and techniques related to Promise
- Abstraction of responses and permissions in a web application
- Modularizing a project to scale
- Other useful asynchronous techniques

 Again, due to the limited length, some of the related code is aggressively simplified and nothing more than the idea itself can be applied practically.

Promise-based web architecture

To have a better understanding of the differences between Promises and traditional callbacks, consider an asynchronous task like this:

```
function process(callback) {
  stepOne((error, resultOne) => {
    if (error) {
      callback(error);
       return;
      }

  stepTwo(resultOne, (error, resultTwo) => {
    if (error) {
      callback(error);
        return;
    }

    callback(undefined, resultTwo + 1);
    });
  });
}
```

If we write preceding above in Promise style, it would be as follows:

```
function process() {
  return stepOne()
    .then(result => stepTwo(result))
.then(result => result + 1);
}
```

As in the preceding example, Promise makes it easy and *natural* to write asynchronous operations with a flat chain instead of nested callbacks. But the most exciting thing about Promise might be the benefits it brings to error handling. In a Promise-based architecture, throwing an error can be safe and pleasant. You don't have to explicitly handle errors when chaining asynchronous operations, and this makes mistakes less likely to happen.

With the growing usage with ES6 compatible runtimes, Promise is already there out of the box. And we actually have plenty of polyfills for Promises (including my *ThenFail* written in TypeScript), as people who write JavaScript roughly refer to the same group of people who created wheels.

Promises work well with other Promises:

- A *Promises/A+* -compatible implementation should work with other *Promises/A+* -compatible implementations
- Promises work best in a Promise-based architecture

If you are new to Promise, you might be complaining about using Promises with a callback-based project. Using asynchronous helpers such as `Promise.each` (non-standard) provided by Promise libraries is a common reason for people to try out Promise, but it turns out they have better alternatives (for a callback-based project) such as the popular `async` library.

The reason that makes you decide to switch should not be these helpers (as there are a lot of them for old-school callbacks as well), but an easier way to handle errors or to take advantage of the ES `async/await` feature, which is based on Promise.

Promisifying existing modules or libraries

Though Promises do best in a Promise-based architecture, it is still possible to begin using Promise with a smaller scope by promisifying existing modules or libraries.

Let's take Node.js style callbacks as an example:

```
import * as FS from 'fs';

FS.readFile('some-file.txt', 'utf-8', (error, text) => {
  if (error) {
    console.error(error);
    return;
  }

  console.log('Content:', text);
});
```

You may expect a promisified version of the `readFile` function to look like the following:

```
FS
  .readFile('some-file.txt', 'utf-8')
  .then(text => {
    console.log('Content:', text);
  })
  .catch(reason => {
    Console.error(reason);
  });
```

The implementation of the promisified function `readFile` can be easy:

```
function readFile(path: string, options: any): Promise<string> {
  return new Promise((resolve, reject) => {
    FS.readFile(path, options, (error, result) => {
      if (error) {
        reject(error);
      } else {
        resolve(result);
      }
    });
  });
}
```

 I am using the type `any` here for parameter options to reduce the size of the code example, but I would suggest not using `any` whenever possible in practice.

There are libraries that are able to promisify methods automatically. Though, unfortunately, you might need to write declaration files yourself for the promisified methods if there are no promisified version available.

Views and controllers in Express

Many of us may have already worked with frameworks such as **Express**. And this is how we render a view or response with JSON in Express:

```
import * as Path from 'path';
import * as express from 'express';

let app = express();

app.set('engine', 'hbs');
app.set('views', Path.join(__dirname, '../views'));

app.get('/page', (req, res) => {
  res.render('page', {
    title: 'Hello, Express!',
    content: '...'
  });
});

app.get('/data', (req, res) => {
  res.json({
```

```
      version: '0.0.0',
      items: []
    });
  });

  app.listen(1337);
```

We will usually separate controllers from the routing configuration:

```
import { Request, Response } from 'express';

export function page(req: Request, res: Response): void {
  res.render('page', {
    title: 'Hello, Express!',
    content: '...'
  });
}
```

Thus we may have a better idea of existing routes, and have controllers managed more easily. Furthermore, automated routing could be introduced so that we don't always need to update routing manually:

```
import * as glob from 'glob';

let controllersDir = Path.join(__dirname, 'controllers');

let controllerPaths = glob.sync('**/*.js', {
    cwd: controllersDir
});

for (let path of controllerPaths) {
    let controller = require(Path.join(controllersDir, path));
    let urlPath = path.replace(/\\/g, '/').replace(/\.js$/, '');

    for (let actionName of Object.keys(controller)) {
        app.get(
            `/${urlPath}/${actionName}`,
            controller[actionName]
        );
    }
}
```

The implementation above is certainly too simple to cover daily use, but it shows a rough idea of how automated routing could work: via conventions based on file structures.

Now, if we are working with asynchronous code written in Promises, an action in the controller could be like the following:

```
export function foo(req: Request, res: Response): void {
    Promise
        .all([
            Post.getContent(),
            Post.getComments()
        ])
        .then(([post, comments]) => {
            res.render('foo', {
                post,
                comments
            });
        });
}
```

 We are destructuring an array within a parameter. `Promise.all` returns a Promise of an array with elements corresponding to the values of the resolvables passed in. (A resolvable means a normal value or a Promise-like object that may resolve to a normal value.)

But that's not enough; we still need to handle errors properly, or in some Promise implementations, the preceding code may fail in silence because the Promise chain is not handled by a rejection handler (which is terrible). In Express, when an error occurs, you should call `next` (the third argument passed into the callback) with the error object:

```
import { Request, Response, NextFunction } from 'express';

export function foo(
  req: Request,
  res: Response,
  next: NextFunction
): void {
  Promise
    // ...
    .catch(reason => next(reason));
}
```

Now, we are fine with the correctness of this approach, but that's simply not how Promises work. Explicit error handling with callbacks could be eliminated in the scope of controllers, and the easiest way is to return the Promise chain and hand over to code that was previously doing routing logic. So the controller could be written like this:

```
export function foo(req: Request, res: Response) {
  return Promise
    .all([
```

```
        Post.getContent(),
        Post.getComments()
    ])
    .then(([post, comments]) => {
      res.render('foo', {
        post,
        comments
              });
          });
    }
```

But, could we make it even better?

Abstraction of responses

We've already been returning a Promise to tell whether an error occurs. So now the returned Promise indicates the status of the response: success or failure. But why we are still calling `res.render()` for rendering the view? The returned promise object could be the response itself rather than just an error indicator.

Think about the controller again:

```
export class Response { }

export class PageResponse extends Response {
  constructor(view: string, data: any) { }
}

export function foo(req: Request) {
  return Promise
    .all([
      Post.getContent(),
      Post.getComments()
    ])
    .then(([post, comments]) => {
      return new PageResponse('foo', {
        post,
        comments
      });
    });
}
```

The response object returned could vary for different response outputs. For example, it could be either a `PageResponse` like it is in the preceding example, a `JSONResponse`, a `StreamResponse`, or even a simple `Redirection`.

As, in most cases, `PageResponse` or `JSONResponse` is applied, and the view of a `PageResponse` can usually be implied by the controller path and action name, it is useful to have those two responses automatically generated from a plain data object with a proper view to render with:

```
export function foo(req: Request) {
  return Promise
    .all([
      Post.getContent(),
      Post.getComments()
    ])
    .then(([post, comments]) => {
      return {
        post,
        comments
      };
    });
}
```

And that's how a Promise-based controller should respond. With this idea, let's update the routing code with the abstraction of responses. Previously, we were passing controller actions directly as Express request handlers. Now we need to do some wrapping up with the actions by resolving the return value, and applying operations based on the resolved result:

1. If it fulfils and it's an instance of `Response`, apply it to the `res` object passed in by Express.
2. If it fulfils and it's a plain object, construct a `PageResponse` or a `JSONResponse` if no view found and apply it to the `res` object.
3. If it rejects, call the `next` function with the reason.

Previously, it was like this:

```
app.get(`/${urlPath}/${actionName}`, controller[actionName]);
```

Now it gets a few more lines:

```
let action = controller[actionName];

app.get(`/${urlPath}/${actionName}`, (req, res, next) => {
  Promise
    .resolve(action(req))
    .then(result => {
      if (result instanceof Response) {
        result.applyTo(res);
```

```
      } else if (existsView(actionName)) {
        new PageResponse(actionName, result).applyTo(res);
      } else {
        new JSONResponse(result).applyTo(res);
      }
    })
    .catch(reason => next(reason));
});
```

However, so far we can handle only GET requests as we hardcoded app.get() in our router implementation. The poor view-matching logic can hardly be used in practice either. We need to make the actions configurable, and ES decorators could do nice work here:

```
export default class Controller {
  @get({
    view: 'custom-view-path'
  })
    foo(req: Request) {
      return {
        title: 'Action foo',
        content: 'Content of action foo'
      };
    }
}
```

I'll leave the implementation to you, and feel free to make it awesome.

Abstraction of permissions

Permissions play an important role in a project, especially in systems that have different user groups, for example, a forum. The abstraction of permissions should be extendable to satisfy changing requirements, and it should be easy to use as well.

Here, we are going to talk about the abstraction of permission in the level of controller actions. Consider the legibility of performing one or more actions as a *privilege*. The permission of a user may consist of several privileges and usually most users at the same level would have the same set of privileges. So we may have a larger concept, namely *groups*.

The abstraction could either work based on both groups and privileges or based on privileges only (groups are then just aliases to sets of privileges):

- Abstractions that validate based on privileges and groups at the same time is easier to build. You do not need to create a large list of which actions can be performed for a certain group of users; granular privileges are only required when necessary.

- Abstractions that validate based on privileges have better control and more flexibility for describing the permission. For example, you can remove a small set of privileges from the permission of a user easily.

However, both approaches have similar upper-level abstractions and differ mostly in implementation. The general structure of the permission abstractions we've talked about is as follows:

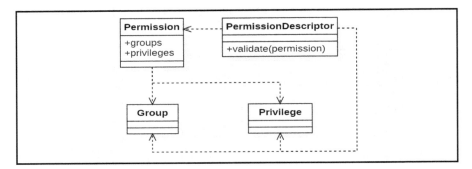

The participants include the following:

- **Privilege**: Describes detailed privileges corresponding to specific actions
- **Group**: Defines a set of privileges
- **Permission**: Describes what a user is capable of doing; consists of groups the user belongs to and privileges the user has
- **Permission descriptor**: Describes how the permission of a user would be sufficient; consists of *possible* groups and privileges

Expected errors

A great concern wiped away by using Promises is that we do not need to worry about throwing an error in a `callback` would crash the application most of the time. The error will flow through the Promises chain and, if not caught, will be handled by our router. Errors can be roughly divided into expected errors and unexpected errors. Expected errors are usually caused by incorrect input or foreseeable exceptions, and unexpected errors are usually caused by bugs or other libraries the project relies on.

For expected errors, we usually want to give user-friendly responses with readable error messages and codes, so that users can help themselves to find solutions or report to us with useful context. For unexpected errors, we would also want reasonable responses (usually messages described as unknown errors), a detailed server-side log (including the real error name, message, stack information, and so on), and even alarms for getting the team notified as soon as possible.

Defining and throwing expected errors

The router will need to handle different types of errors, and an easy way to achieve that is to subclass a universal `ExpectedError` class and throw its instances out:

```
import ExtendableError from 'extendable-error';

class ExpectedError extends ExtendableError {
  constructor(
    message: string,
    public code: number
  ) {
    super(message);
  }
}
```

 The `extendable-error` is a package of mine that handles stack trace and the `message` property. You can directly extend the `Error` class as well.

Thus, when receiving an expected error, we can safely output its message as part of the response. And if it's not an instance of `ExpectedError`, we can then output predefined `unknown` error messages and have detailed error information logged.

Transforming errors

Some errors, such as those caused by unstable networks or remote services, are expected; we may want to catch those errors and throw them out again as expected errors. But it is rather trivial to actually do that. A centralized error-transforming process can then be applied to reduce the efforts required to manage those errors.

The transforming process includes two parts: filtering (or matching) and transforming. There are many approaches to filter errors, such as the following:

- **Filter by error class**: Many third-party libraries throw errors of certain classes. Taking Sequelize (a popular Node.js ORM) as an example, it throws `DatabaseError, ConnectionError, ValidationError`, and so on. By filtering errors by checking whether they are instances of a certain error class, we may easily pick up target errors from the pile.
- **Filter by string or regular expression**: Sometimes a library might be throwing errors that are instances of an `Error` class itself instead of its subclasses; this makes those errors harder to distinguish from others. In this situation, we may filter those errors by their message, with keywords or regular expressions.
- **Filter by scope**: It's possible that instances of the same error class with the same error message should result in different responses. One of the reasons might be that the operation that throws a certain error is at a lower level, but is being used by upper structures within different scopes. Thus, a `scope` mark could be added for those errors and make them easier to be filtered.

There could be more ways to filter errors, and they are usually able to cooperate as well. By properly applying those filters and transforming errors, we can reduce noise for analyzing what's going on within a system and locate problems faster if they show up.

Modularizing project

Before ES6, there were a lot of module solutions for JavaScript that worked. The two most famous of them are AMD and commonjs. AMD is designed for asynchronous module loading, which is mostly applied in browsers, while commonjs does module loading synchronously, and that's the way the Node.js module system works.

To make it work asynchronously, writing an AMD module takes more characters. And due to the popularity of tools such as browserify and webpack, commonjs becomes popular even for browser projects.

The proper granularity of internal modules could help a project keep its structure healthy. Consider a project structure like this:

```
project
├─controllers
├─core
│ │ index.ts
│ │
```

```
|    ├──product
|    |    index.ts
|    |    order.ts
|    |    shipping.ts
|    |
|    └──user
|         index.ts
|         account.ts
|         statistics.ts
|
├──helpers
├──models
├──utils
└──views
```

Assume we are writing a controller file that's going to import a module defined by the `core/product/order.ts` file. Previously, with the commonjs `require` style, we would want to write the following:

```
const Order = require('../core/product/order');
```

Now, with the new ES `import` syntax, it would be as follows:

```
import * as Order from '../core/product/order';
```

Wait, isn't that essentially the same? Sort of. But you may have noticed several `index.ts` files I've put into folders. Now, in the file `core/product/index.ts`, we can have the following:

```
import * as Order from './order';
import * as Shipping from './shipping';

export { Order, Shipping }
```

Alternatively, we could have the following:

```
export * from './order';
export * from './shipping';
```

What's the difference? The ideas behind those two approaches of re-exporting modules can vary. The first style works better when we treat `Order` and `Shipping` as namespaces, under which the entity names may not be easy to distinguish from one group to another. With this style, the files are the natural boundaries of building those namespaces. The second style weakens the namespace property of two files and uses them as tools to organize objects and classes under the same larger category.

A good thing about using those files as namespaces is that multiple-level re-exporting is fine while weakening namespaces makes it harder to understand different identifier names as the number of re-exporting levels grows.

Asynchronous patterns

When we are writing JavaScript with network or file system I/O, there is a 95% chance that we are doing it asynchronously. However, an asynchronous code may tremendously decrease the determinability at the dimension of time. But we are so lucky that JavaScript is usually single-threaded; this makes it possible for us to write predictable code without mechanisms such as locks most of the time.

Writing predictable code

The predictable code relies on predictable tools (if you are using any). Consider a helper like this:

```
type Callback = () => void;

let isReady = false;
let callbacks: Callback[] = [];

setTimeout(() => {
  callbacks.forEach(callback => callback());
  callbacks = undefined;
  }, 100);
export function ready(callback: Callback): void {
  if (!callbacks) {
    callback();
  } else {
    callbacks.push(callback);
  }
}
```

This module exports a `ready` function, which will invoke the callbacks passed in when "ready". It will assure that callbacks will be called even if added after that. However, you cannot say for sure whether the callback will be called in the current event loop:

```
import { ready } from './foo';

let i = 0;

ready(() => {
```

```
    console.log(i);
});

i++;
```

In the preceding example, i could either be 0 or 1 when the callback gets called. Again, this is not wrong, or even bad, it just makes the code less predictable. When someone else reads this piece of code, he or she will need to consider two possibilities of how this program would run. To avoid this issue, we can simply wrap up the synchronous invocation with setImmediate (it may fallback to setTimeout in older browsers):

```
export function ready(callback: Callback): void {
    if (!callbacks) {
        setImmediate(() => callback());
    } else {
        callbacks.push(callback);
    }
}
```

Writing predictable code is actually more than writing predictable asynchronous code. The highlighted line above can also be written as setImmediate(callback), but that would make people who read your code think twice: how will callback get called and what are the arguments?

Consider the line of code below:

```
let results = ['1', '2', '3'].map(parseInt);
```

What's the value of the array results? Certainly not [1, 2, 3]. Because the callback passed to the method map receives several arguments: value of current item, index of current item, and the whole array, while the function parseInt accepts two arguments: string to parse, and radix. So results are actually the results of the following snippet:

```
[parseInt('1', 0), parseInt('2', 1), parseInt('3', 2)];
```

However, it is actually okay to write setImmediate(callback) directly, as the APIs of those functions (including setTimeout, setInterval, process.nextTick, and so on) are designed to be used in this way. And it is fair to assume people who are going to maintain this project know that as well. But for other asynchronous functions whose signatures are not well known, it is recommended to call them with explicit arguments.

Asynchronous creational patterns

We talked about many creational patterns in Chapter 3, *Creational Design Patterns*. While a constructor cannot be asynchronous, some of those patterns may have problems applying to asynchronous scenarios. But others need only slight modifications for asynchronous use.

In Chapter 4, *Structural Design Patterns* we walked through the Adapter Pattern with a storage example that opens the database and creates a storage object asynchronously:

```
class Storage {
  private constructor() { }

  open(): Promise<Storage> {
    return openDatabase()
      .then(db => new Storage(db))
  }
}
```

And in the Proxy Pattern, we made the storage object immediately available from its constructor. When a method of the object is called, it waits for the initialization to complete and finishes the operation:

```
class Storage {
  private dbPromise: Promise<IDBDatabase>;

  get dbReady(): Promise<IDBDatabase> {
    if (this.dbPromise) {
      return this.dbPromise;
    }
    // ...      }

  get<T>(): Promise<T> {
    return this
      .dbReady
      .then(db => {
        // ...
      });
  }
}
```

A drawback of this approach is that all members that rely on initialization have to be asynchronous, though most of the time they just are asynchronous.

Asynchronous middleware and hooks

The concept of middleware is widely used in frameworks such as Express. Middleware usually processes its target in serial. In Express, middleware is applied roughly in the order it is added while there are not different phases. Some other frameworks, however, provide hooks for different phases in time. For example, there are hooks that will be triggered *before install*, *after install*, *after uninstall*, and so on.

 The middleware mechanism of Express is actually a variant of the Chain of Responsibility Pattern. And depending on the specific middleware to be used, it can act more or less like hooks instead of a responsibility chain.

The reasons to implement middleware or hooks vary. They may include the following:

- **Extensibility**: Most of the time, they are applied due to the requirement of extensibility. New rules and processes could be easily added by new middleware or hooks.
- **Decoupling interactions with business logic**: A module that should only care about business logic could need potential interactions with an interface. For example, we might expect to be able to either enter or update credentials while processing an operation, without restarting everything. Thus we can create a middleware or a hook, so that we don't need to have them tightly coupled.

The implementation of asynchronous middleware could be interesting. Take the Promise version as an example:

```
type Middleware = (host: Host) => Promise<void>;

class Host {
  middlewares: Middleware[] = [];

  start(): Promise<void> {
    return this
      .middlewares
      .reduce((promise, middleware) => {
        return promise.then(() => middleware(this));
      }, Promise.resolve());
  }
}
```

Here, we're using `reduce` to do the trick. We passed in a Promise fulfilled with undefined as the initial value, and chained it with the result of `middleware(this)`. And this is actually how the `Promise.each` helper is implemented in many Promise libraries.

Event-based stream parser

When creating an application relies on socket, we usually need a lightweight "protocol" for the client and server to communicate. Unlike XHR that already handles everything, by using socket, you will need to define the boundaries so data won't be mixed up.

Data transferred through a socket might be concatenated or split, but TCP connection ensures the order and correctness of bytes gets transferred. Consider a tiny protocol that consists of only two parts: a 4-byte unsigned integer followed by a JSON string with byte length that matches the 4-byte unsigned integer.

For example, for JSON "{}", the data packet would be as follows:

```
Buffer <00 00 00 02 7b 7d>
```

To build such a data packet, we just need to convert the JSON string to `Buffer` (with encoding such as `utf-8`, which is default encoding for Node.js), and then prepend its length:

```
function buildPacket(data: any): Buffer {
    let json = JSON.stringify(data);
    let jsonBuffer = new Buffer(json);

    let packet = new Buffer(4 + jsonBuffer.length);

    packet.writeUInt32BE(jsonBuffer.length, 0);
    jsonBuffer.copy(packet, 4, 0);

    return packet;
}
```

A socket client emits a `data` event when it receives new buffers. Assume we are going to send the following JSON strings:

```
// 00 00 00 02 7b 7d
{}

// 00 00 00 0f 7b 22 6b 65 79 22 3a 22 76 61 6c 75 65 22 7d
{"key":"value"}
```

We may be receiving them like this:

- Get two buffers separately; each of them is a complete packet with length and JSON bytes

- Get one single buffer with two buffers concatenated
- Get two, or more than two, buffers; at least one of the previously sent packets gets split into several ones.

The entire process is happening asynchronously. But just like the socket client emits a `data` event, the parser can just emit its own `data` event when a complete packet gets parsed. The parser for parsing our tiny protocol may have only two states, corresponding to header (JSON byte length) and body (JSON bytes), and the emitting of the `data` event happens after successfully parsing the body:

```
class Parser extends EventEmitter {
  private buffer = new Buffer(0);
  private state = State.header;

  append(buffer: Buffer): void {
    this.buffer = Buffer.concat([this.buffer, buffer]);
    this.parse();
  }

  private parse(): void { }

  private parseHeader(): boolean { }

  private parseBody(): boolean { }
}
```

Due to the limitation of length, I'm not going to put the complete implementation of the parser here. For the complete code, please refer to the file `src/event-based-parser.ts` in the code bundle of `Chapter 7`, *Patterns and Architectures in JavaScript and TypeScript*.

Thus the use of such a parser could be as follows:

```
import * as Net from 'net';

let parser = new Parser();
let client = Net.connect(port);

client.on('data', (data: Buffer) => {
  parser.append(data);
});

parser.on('data', (data: any) => {
  console.log('Data received:', data);
});
```

Summary

In this chapter, we discussed some interesting ideas and an architecture formed by those ideas. Most of the topics focus on a small scope and do their own job, but there are also ideas about putting a whole system together.

The code that implements techniques such as expected error and the approach to managing modules in a project is not hard to apply. But with proper application, it can bring notable convenience to the entire project.

However, as I have already mentioned at the beginning of this chapter, there are too many beautiful things in JavaScript and TypeScript to be covered or even mentioned in a single chapter. Please don't stop here, and keep exploring.

Many patterns and architectures are the result of some fundamental principles in software engineering. Those principles might not always be applicable in every scenario, but they may help when you feel confused. In the next chapter, we are going to talk about SOLID principles in object-oriented design and find out how those principles may help form a useful pattern.

8
SOLID Principles

SOLID Principles are well-known Object-Oriented Design (**OOD**)principles summarized by Uncle Bob (Robert C. Martin). The word SOLID comes from the initials of the five principles it refers to, including **Single responsibility principle**, **Open-closed principle**, **Liskov substitution principle**, **Interface segregation principle** and **Dependency inversion principle**. Those principles are closely related to each other, and can be a great guidance in practice.

Here is a widely used summary of SOLID principles from Uncle Bob:

- **Single responsibility principle**: A class should have one, and only one, reason to change
- **Open-closed principle**: You should be able to extend a classes behavior, without modifying it
- **Liskov substitution principle**: Derived classes must be substitutable for their base classes
- **Interface segregation principle**: Make fine-grained interfaces that are client specific
- **Dependency inversion principle**: Depend on abstractions, not on concretions

In this chapter, we will walk through them and find out how those principles can help form a design that *smells* nice.

But before we proceed, I want to mention that a few of the reasons why those principles exist might be related to the age in which they were raised, the languages and their building or distributing process people were working with, and even computing resources. When being applied to JavaScript and TypeScript projects nowadays, some of the details may not be necessary. Think more about what problems those principles want to prevent people from getting into, rather than the literal descriptions of how a principle should be followed.

Single responsibility principle

The single responsibility principle declares that a class should have one, and only one reason to change. And the definition of the world *reason* in this sentence is important.

Example

Consider a `Command` class that is designed to work with both command-line interface and graphical user interface:

```
class Command {
  environment: Environment;

  print(items: ListItem[]) {
    let stdout = this.environment.stdout;
    stdout.write('Items:\n');
    for (let item of items) {
      stdout.write(item.text + '\n');
    }
  }
  render(items: ListItem[]) {
    let element = <List items={items}></List>;
    this.environment.render(element);
  }
  execute() { }
}
```

To make this actually work, `execute` method would need to handle both the command execution and result displaying:

```
class Command {
  ..
  execute() {
  let items = ...;
    if (this.environment.type === 'cli') {
      this.print(items);
    } else {
      this.render(items);
    }
  }
}
```

In this example, there are two reasons for changes:

1. How a command gets executed.
2. How the result of a command gets displayed in different environments.

Those reasons lead to changes in different dimensions and violate the single responsibility principle. This might result in a messy situation over time. A better solution is to have those two responsibilities separated and managed by the CommandEnvironment:

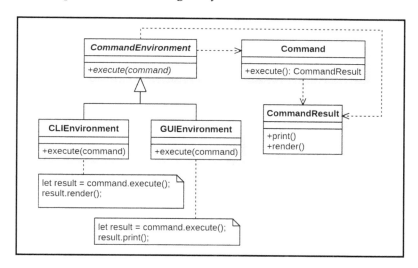

Does this look familiar to you? Because it is a variant of the Visitor Pattern. Now it is the environment that executes a specific command and handles its result based on a concrete environment class.

Choosing an axis

You might be thinking, doesn't CommandResult violate the single responsibility principle by having the abilities to display content in a different environment? Yes, and no. When the axis of this reason is set to displaying content, it does not; but if the axis is set to displaying in a specific environment, it does. But take the overall structure into consideration, the result of a command is expected to be an output that can adapt to a different environment. And thus the reason is one-dimensional and confirms the principle.

Open-closed principle

The open-closed principle declares that you should be able to extend a class' behavior, without modifying it. This principle is raised by Bertrand Meyer in 1988:

> *Software entities (classes, modules, functions, etc.) should be open for extension, but closed for modification.*

A program depends on all the entities it uses, that means changing the already-being-used part of those entities may just crash the entire program. So the idea of the open-closed principle is straightforward: we'd better have entities that never change in any way other than extending itself.

That means once a test is written and passing, ideally, it should never be changed for newly added features (and it needs to keep passing, of course). Again, ideally.

Example

Consider an API hub that handles HTTP requests to and responses from the server. We are going to have several files written as modules, including `http-client.ts`, `hub.ts` and `app.ts` (but we won't actually write `http-client.ts` in this example, you will need to use some imagination).

Save the code below as file `hub.ts`.

```
import { HttpClient, HttpResponse } from './http-client';

export function update(): Promise<HttpResponse> {
  let client = new HttpClient();
  return client.get('/api/update');
}
```

And save the code below as file `app.ts`.

```
import Hub from './hub';

Hub
  .update()
  .then(response => JSON.stringify(response.text))
  .then(result => {
    console.log(result);
});
```

Bravely done! Now we have `app.ts` badly coupled with `http-client.ts`. And if we want to adapt this API hub to something like WebSocket, BANG.

So how can we create entities that are open for extension, but closed for modification? The key is a *stable abstraction that adapts.* Consider the storage and client example we took with Adapter Pattern in `Chapter 4`, *Structural Design Patterns* we had a `Storage` interface that isolates implementation of database operations from the client. And assuming that the interface is well-designed to meet upcoming feature requirements, it is possible that it will never change or just need to be extended during the life cycle of the program.

Abstraction in JavaScript and TypeScript

Guess what, our beloved JavaScript does not have an interface, and it is dynamically typed. We were not even able to actually write an interface. However, we could still write down documentation about the abstraction and create new concrete implementations just by obeying that description.

But TypeScript offers interface, and we can certainly take advantage of it. Consider the `CommandResult` class in the previous section. We were writing it as a concrete class, but it may have subclasses that override the `print` or `render` method for customized output. However, the type system in TypeScript cares only about the shape of a type. That means, while you are declaring an entity with type `CommandResult`, the entity does not need to be an instance of `CommandResult`: any object with a compatible type (namely has methods `print` and `render` with proper signatures in this case) will do the job.

For example, the following code is valid:

```
let environment: Environment;

let command: Command = {
  environment,
  print(items) { },
  render(items) { },
  execute() { }
};
```

Refactor earlier

I double stressed that the open-closed principle can only be perfectly followed under ideal scenarios. That can be a result of two reasons:

1. *Not all entities in a system can be open to extension and closed to modification at the same time.* There will always be changes that need to break the closure of existing entities to complete their functionalities. When we are designing the interfaces, we need different strategies for creating stable closures for different foreseeable situations. But this requires notable experience and no one can do it perfectly.

2. *None of us is too good at designing a program that lasts long and stays healthy forever.* Even with thorough consideration, abstractions designed at the beginning can be choppy facing the changing requirements.

So when we are expecting the entities to be closed for modification, it does not mean that we should just stand there and watch it being closed. Instead, when things are still under control, we should refactor and *keep the abstraction in the status of being open to extension and closed to modification* at the time point of refactoring.

Liskov substitution principle

The open-closed principle is the essential principle of keeping code maintainable and reusable. And the key to the open-closed principle is abstraction with polymorphism. Behaviors like implementing interfaces, or extending classes make polymorphic *shapes*, but that might not be enough.

The Liskov substitution principle declares that derived classes must be substitutable for their base classes. Or in the words of Barbara Liskov, who raised this principle:

> *What is wanted here is something like the following substitution property: If for each object o1 of type S there is an object o2 of type T such that for all programs P defined in terms of T, the behavior of P is unchanged when o1 is substituted for o2 then S is a subtype of T.*

Never mind. Let's try another one: *any foreseeable usage of the instance of a class should be working with the instances of its derived classes.*

Example

And here we go with a straightforward violation example. Consider `Noodles` and `InstantNoodles` (a subclass of `Noodles`) to be cooked:

```
function cookNoodles(noodles: Noodles) {
  if (noodles instanceof InstantNoodles) {
    cookWithBoiledWaterAndBowl(noodles);
  } else {
    cookWithWaterAndBoiler(noodles);
  }
}
```

Now if we want to have some fried noodles... The `cookNoodles` function does not seem to be capable of handling that. Clearly, this violates the Liskov substitution principle, though it does not mean that it's a bad design.

Let's consider another example written by Uncle Bob in his article talking about this principle. We are creating class `Square` which is a subclass of `Rectangle`, but instead of adding new features, it adds a constraint to `Rectangle`: the width and height of a square should always be equal to each other. Assume we have a `Rectangle` class that allows its width and height to be set:

```
class Rectangle {
  constructor(
    private _width: number;
    private _height: number;
  ) { }
  set width(value: number) {
    this._width = value;
  }
  set height(value: number) {
    this._height = value;
  }
}
```

Now we have a problem with its subclass `Square`, because it gets `width` and `height` setters from `Rectangle` while it shouldn't. We can certainly override those setters and make both of them update width and height simultaneously. But in some situations, the client might just not want that, because doing so will make the program harder to be predicted.

The `Square` and `Rectangle` example violates the Liskov substitution principle. Not because we didn't find a good way to inherit, but because `Square` does not conform the behavior of `Rectangle` and should not be a subclass of it at the beginning.

The constraints of substitution

Type is an important part in a programming language, even in JavaScript. But having the same *shape*, being on the same hierarchy does not mean they can be the substitution of another without some pain. More than just the *shape*, the complete behavior is what really matters for implementations that hold to the Liskov substitution principle.

Interface segregation principle

We've already discussed the important role played by abstractions in object-oriented design. The abstractions and their derived classes without separation usually come up with hierarchical tree structures. That means when you choose to create a branch, you create a parallel abstraction to all of those on another branch.

For a family of classes with only one level of inheritance, this is not a problem: because it is just what you want to have those classes derived from. But for a hierarchy with greater depth, it could be.

Example

Consider the `TextReader` example we took with Template Method Pattern in Chapter 6, *Behavioral Design Patterns: Continuous* we had `FileAsciiTextReader` and `HttpAsciiTextReader` derived from `AsciiTextReader`. But what if we want to have other readers that understand UTF-8 encoding?

To achieve that goal, we have two common options: separate the interface into two for different objects that cooperate, or separate the interface into two then get them implemented by a single class.

For the first case, we can refactor the code with two abstractions, `BytesReader` and `TextReader`:

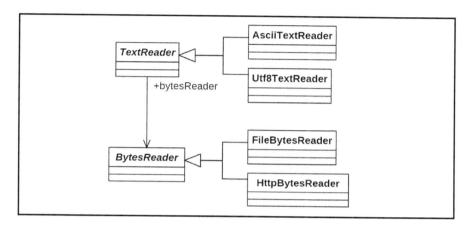

And for the second case, we can separate method `readAllBytes` and `decodeBytes` onto two interfaces, for example, `BytesReader` and `BytesDecoder`. Thus we may implement them separately and use techniques like mixin to put them together:

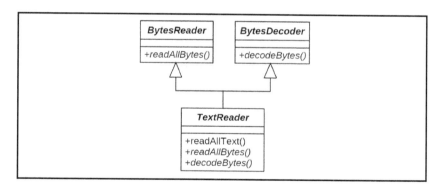

An interesting point about this example is that `TextReader` above itself is an abstract class. To make this mixin actually work, we need to create a concrete class of `TextReader` (without actually implementing `readAllBytes` and `decodeBytes`), and then mixin two concrete classes of `BytesReader` and `BytesDecoder`.

Proper granularity

It is said that by creating smaller interfaces, we can avoid a client from using big classes with features that it never needs. This may cause unnecessary usage of resources, but in practice, that usually won't be a problem. The most important part of the interface segregation principle is still about keeping code maintainable and reusable.

Then the question comes out again, how small should an interface be? I don't think I have a simple answer for that. But I am sure that being too small might not help.

Dependency inversion principle

When we talk about dependencies, the natural sense is about dependencies from bottom to top, just like how buildings are built. But unlike a building that stands for tens of years with little change, software keeps changing during its life cycle. Every change costs, more or less.

The dependency inversion principle declares that entities should depend on abstractions, not on concretions. Higher level code should not depend directly on low-level implementations, instead, it should depend on abstractions that *lead to* those implementations. And this is why things are *inverse*.

Example

Still taking the HTTP client and API hub as an example, which obviously violates the dependency inversion principle, taking the foreseeable application into consideration, what the API hub should depend on is a messaging mechanism bridging client and server, but not bare HTTP client. This means we should have an abstraction layer of messaging before the concrete implementation of HTTP client:

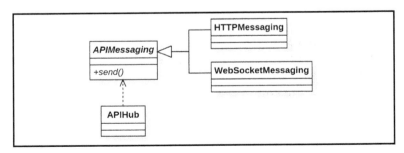

Separating layers

Compared to other principles discussed in this chapter, the dependency inversion principle cares more about the scope of modules or packages. As the abstraction might usually be more stable than concrete implementations, by following dependency inversion principle, we can minimize the impact from low-level changes to higher level behaviors.

But for JavaScript (or TypeScript) projects as the language is dynamically typed, this principle is more about an idea of guidance that leads to a stable abstraction between different layers of code implementation.

Originally, an important benefit of following this principle is that, if modules or packages are relatively larger, separating them by abstraction could save a lot of time in compilation. But for JavaScript, we don't have to worry about that; and for TypeScript, we don't have to recompile the entire project for making changes to separated modules either.

Summary

In this chapter, we walked through the well-known SOLID principles with simple examples. Sometimes, following those principles could lead us to a useful design pattern. And we also found that those principles are strongly bound to each other. Usually violating one of them may indicate other violations.

Those principles could be extremely helpful for OOD, but could also be overkill if they are applied without proper adaptions. A well-designed system should have those principles confirmed just right, or it might harm.

In the next chapter, instead of theories, we'll have more time with a complete workflow with testing and continuous integration involved.

9
The Road to Enterprise Application

After walking through common design patterns, we have now the basis of code designing. However, software engineering is more about writing beautiful code. While we are trying to keep the code healthy and robust, we still have a lot to do to keep the project and the team healthy, robust, and ready to scale. In this chapter, we'll talk about popular elements in the workflow of web applications, and how to design a workflow that fits your team.

The first part would be setting up the build steps of our demo project. We'll quickly walk through how to build frontend projects with *webpack*, one of the most popular packaging tools these days. And we'll configure tests, code linter, and then set up continuous integration.

There are plenty of nice choices when it comes to workflow integration. Personally, I prefer Team Foundation Server for private projects or a combination of GitHub and Travis-CI for open-source projects. While Team Foundation Server (or Visual Studio Team Services as its cloud-based version) provides a one-stop solution for the entire application life cycle, the combination of GitHub and Travis-CI is more popular in the JavaScript community. In this chapter, we are going use the services provided by GitHub and Travis-CI for our workflow.

Here are what we are going to walk through:

- Packaging frontend assets with webpack.
- Setting up tests and linter.
- Getting our hands on a Git flow branching model and other Git-related workflow.
- Connecting a GitHub repository with Travis-CI.
- A peek into automated deployment.

Creating an application

We've talked about creating TypeScript applications for both frontend and backend projects in the `Chapter 1`, *Tools and Frameworks*. And now we are going to create an application that contains two TypeScript projects at the same time.

Decision between SPA and "normal" web applications

Applications for different purposes result in different choices. SPA (single page application) usually delivers a better user experience after being loaded, but it can also lead to trade-offs on SEO and may rely on more complex MV* frameworks like Angular.

One solution to build SEO-friendly SPA is to build a universal (or isomorphic) application that runs the *same* code on both frontend and backend, but that could introduce even more complexity. Or a reverse proxy could be configured to render automatically generated pages with the help of tools like *Phantom*.

In this demo project, we'll choose a more traditional web application with multiple pages to build. And here's the file structure of the client project:

```
project
| package.json
|
|─client
|  | tsconfig.json
|  |
|  |─src
|  |  |─ common
|  |  |─ pages
|  |        |─ default
|  |        |    |─ default.hbs
|  |        |    |─ default.scss
|  |        |    |─ default.ts
|  |        |
|  |        |─ account
|  |             |─ account.hbs
|  |             |─ account.scss
|  |             |─ account.ts
|  |
|  |─out
|
|─server
|─node_modules
```

Taking team collaboration into consideration

Before we actually start creating a real-world application, we need to come up with a reasonable application structure. A proper application structure is more than something under which the code compiles and runs. It should be a result, taking how your team members work together into consideration.

For example, a naming convention is involved in this demo client structure shown earlier: page assets are named after page names instead of their types (for example, `style.scss`) or names like `index.ts`. And the consideration behind this convention is making it more friendly for file navigation by the keyboard.

Of course, this consideration is valid only if a significant number of developers in your team are cool with keyboard navigation. Other than operation preferences, the experiences and backgrounds of a team should be seriously considered as well:

- Should the "full-stack" mode be enabled for your team?
- Should the "full-stack" mode be enabled for every engineer in your team?
- How should you divide work between frontend and backend?

Usually, it's not necessary and not efficient to limit the access of a frontend engineer to client-side development. If it's possible, frontend engineers could take over the controller layer of the backend and leave hardcore business models and logic to engineers that focus more on the backend.

We are having the client and server-side projects in the same repository for an easier integration during development. But it does not mean everything in the frontend or backend code base should be in this single repository. Instead, multiple modules could be extracted and maintained by different developers in practice. For example, you can have database models and business logic models separated from the controllers on the backend.

Building and testing projects

We have already talked about building and testing TypeScript projects at the beginning of this book. In this section, we will go a little bit further for frontend projects, including the basis of using Webpack to load static assets as well as **code linting**.

Static assets packaging with webpack

Modularizing helps code keep a healthy structure and makes it maintainable. However, it could lead to performance issues if development-time code written in *small* modules are directly deployed without bundling for production usage. So static assets packaging becomes a serious topic of frontend engineering.

Back to the old days, packaging JavaScript files was just about *uglifying* source code and concatenating files together. The project might be modularized as well, but in a *global* way. Then we have libraries like Require.js, with modules no longer automatically exposing themselves to the global scope.

But as I have mentioned, having the client download module files separately is not ideal for performance; soon we had tools like browserify, and later, webpack – one of the most popular frontend packaging tools these days.

Introduction to webpack

Webpack is an integrated packaging tool dedicated (at least at the beginning) to frontend projects. It is designed to package not only JavaScript, but also other static assets in a frontend project. Webpack provides built-in support for both **asynchronous module definition** (**AMD**) and commonjs, and can load ES6 or other types of resources via plugins.

 ES6 module support will get built-in for webpack 2.0, but by the time this chapter is written, you still need plugins like `babel-loader` or `ts-loader` to make it work. And of course we are going to use `ts-loader` later.

To install webpack via `npm`, execute the following command:

```
$ npm install webpack -g
```

Bundling JavaScript

Before we actually use webpack to load TypeScript files, we'll have a quick walk through of bundling JavaScript.

First, let's create the file `index.js` under the directory `client/src/` with the following code inside:

```
var Foo = require('./foo');

Foo.test();
```

Then create the file `foo.js` in the same folder with the following content:

```
exports.test = function test() {
  console.log('Hello, Webpack!');
};
```

Now we can have them bundled as a single file using the webpack command-line interface:

$ webpack ./client/src/index.js ./client/out/bundle.js

By viewing the `bundle.js` file generated by webpack, you will see that the contents of both `index.js` and `foo.js` have been wrapped into that single file, together with the bootstrap code of webpack. Of course, we would prefer not to type those file paths in the command line every time, but to use a configuration file instead.

Webpack provides configuration file support in the form of JavaScript files, which makes it more flexible to generate necessary data like bundle entries automatically. Let's create a simple configuration file that does what the previous command did.

Create file `client/webpack.config.js` with the following lines:

```
'use strict';

const Path = require('path');

module.exports = {
  entry: './src/index',
  output: {
    path: Path.join(__dirname, 'out'),
    filename: 'bundle.js'
  }
};
```

These are the two things to mention:

1. The value of the entry field is not the filename, but the *module id* (most of the time this is unresolved) instead. This means that you can have the .js extension omitted, but have to prefix it with ./ or ../ by default when referencing a file.
2. The output path is required to be absolute. Building an absolute path with __dirname ensures it works properly if we are not executing webpack under the same directory as the configuration file.

Loading TypeScript

Now we are going to load and transpile our beloved TypeScript using the webpack plugin ts-loader. Before updating the configuration, let's install the necessary npm packages:

```
$ npm install typescript ts-loader --save-dev
```

If things go well, you should have the TypeScript compiler as well as the ts-loader plugin installed locally. We may also want to rename and update the files index.js and foo.js to TypeScript files.

Rename index.js to index.ts and update the module importing syntax:

```
import * as Foo from './foo';

Foo.test();
```

Rename foo.js to foo.ts and update the module exporting syntax:

```
export function test() {
  console.log('Hello, Webpack!');
}
```

Of course, we would want to add the tsconfig.json file for those TypeScript files (in the folder client):

```
{
  "compilerOptions": {
    "target": "es5",
    "module": "commonjs"
  },
  "exclude": [
    "out",
    "node_modules"
  ]
}
```

The compiler option `outDir` is omitted here because it is managed in the webpack configuration file.

To make webpack work with TypeScript via `ts-loader`, we'll need to tell webpack some information in the configuration file:

1. Webpack will need to resolve files with `.ts` extensions. Webpack has a default extensions list to resolve, including `''` (empty string), `'.webpack.js'`, `'.web.js'`, and `'.js'`. We need to add `'.ts'` to this list for it to recognize TypeScript files.
2. Webpack will need to have `ts-loader` loading `.ts` modules because it does not compile TypeScript itself.

And here is the updated `webpack.config.js`:

```
'use strict';

const Path = require('path');

module.exports = {
  entry: './src/index',
  output: {
    path: Path.join(__dirname, 'bld'),
    filename: 'bundle.js'
  },
  resolve: {
    extensions: ['', '.webpack.js', '.web.js', '.ts', '.js']
  },
  module: {
    loaders: [
      { test: /\.ts$/, loader: 'ts-loader' }
    ]
  }
};
```

Now execute the command `webpack` under the `client` folder again, we should get the compiled and bundled output as expected.

During development, we can enable *transpile mode* (corresponding to the compiler option `isolatedModules`) of TypeScript to have better performance on compiling changing files. But it means we'll need to rely on an IDE or an editor to provide error hints. And remember to make another compilation with transpile mode disabled after debugging to ensure things still work.

To enable transpile mode, add a `ts` field (defined by the `ts-loader` plugin) with `transpileOnly` set to `true`:

```
module.exports = {
  ...
  ts: {
      transpileOnly: true
  }
};
```

Splitting code

To take the advantage of code caching across pages, we might want to split the packaged modules as common pieces. The webpack provides a built-in plugin called `CommonsChunkPlugin` that can pick out common modules and have them packed separately.

For example, if we create another file called `bar.ts` that imports `foo.ts` just like `index.ts` does, `foo.ts` can be treated as a common chunk and be packed separately:

```
module.exports = {
  entry: ['./src/index', './src/bar'],
  ...
  plugins: [
    new Webpack.optimize.CommonsChunkPlugin({
      name: 'common',
      filename: 'common.js'
    })
  ]
};
```

For multi-page applications, it is common to have different pages with different entry scripts. Instead of manually updating the `entry` field in the configuration file, we can take advantage of it being JavaScript and generate proper entries automatically. To do so, we might want the help of the npm package `glob` for matching page entries:

```
$ npm install glob --saved-dev
```

And then update the webpack configuration file:

```
const glob = require('glob');

module.exports = {
  entry: glob
    .sync('./src/pages/*/*.ts')
```

```
  .filter(path =>
    Path.basename(path, '.ts') ===
    Path.basename(Path.dirname(path))
  ),
  ...
};
```

Splitting the code can be rather a complex topic for deep dive, so we'll stop here and let you explore.

Loading other static assets

As we've mentioned, webpack can also be used to load other static assets like stylesheet and its extensions. For example, you can use the combination of `style-loader`, `css-loader` and `sass-loader/less-loader` to load `.sass/.less` files.

The configuration is similar to `ts-loader` so we'll not spend extra pages for their introductions. For more information, refer to the following URLs:

- Embedded stylesheets in webpack:
  `https://webpack.github.io/docs/stylesheets.html`
- SASS loader for webpack: `https://github.com/jtangelder/sass-loader`
- LESS loader for webpack: `https://github.com/webpack/less-loader`

Adding TSLint to projects

A consistent code style is an important factor of code quality, and linters are our best friends when it comes to code styles (and they also helps with common mistakes). For TypeScript linting, TSLint is currently the simplest choice.

The installation and configuration of TSLint are easy. To begin with, let's install `tslint` as a global command:

```
$ npm install tslint -g
```

And then we need to initialize a configuration file using the following command under the project root directory:

```
$ tslint --init
```

TSLint will then generate a default configuration file named `tslint.json`, and you may customize it based on your own preferences. And now we can use it to lint our TypeScript source code:

```
$ tslint */src/**/*.ts
```

Integrating webpack and tslint command with npm scripts

As we've mentioned before, an advantage of using npm scripts is that they can handle local packages with executables properly by adding `node_modules/.bin` to `PATH`. And to make our application easier to build and test for other developers, we can have `webpack` and `tslint` installed as development dependencies and add related scripts to `package.json`:

```
"scripts": {
  "build-client": "cd client && webpack",
  "build-server": "tsc --project server",
  "build": "npm run build-client && npm run build-server",
  "lint": "tslint ./*/src/**/*.ts",
  "test-client": "cd client && mocha",
  "test-server": "cd server && mocha",
  "test": "npm run lint && npm run test-client && npm run test-server"
}
```

Version control

Thinking back to my senior high school days, I knew nothing about version control tools. The best thing I could do was to create a daily archive of my code on a USB disk. And yes I did lose one!

Nowadays, with the boom of version control tools like Git and the availabilities of multiple free services like GitHub and Visual Studio Team Services, managing code with version control tools has become a daily basis for every developer.

As the most popular version control tool, Git has already been playing an important role in your work or personal projects. In this section, we'll talk about popular practices of using Git in a team.

Note that I am assuming that you already have the basic knowledge of Git, and know how to make operations like `init`, `commit`, `push`, `pull` and `merge`. If not, please get hands on and try to understand those operations before continue.

Check out this quick tutorial at: `https://try.github.io/`.

Git flow

Version control plays an important a role and it does not only influence the source code management process but also shapes the entire workflow of product development and delivery. Thus a *successful* branching model becomes a serious choice.

Git flow is a collection of Git extensions that provides high-level repository operations for a branching model raised by Vincent Driessen. The name *Git flow* usually refers to the branching model as well.

In this branching model, there are two main branches: `master` and `develop`, as well as three different types of supporting branches: `feature`, `hotfix`, and `release`.

With the help of Git flow extensions, we can easily apply this branching model without having to remember and type detailed sequences of commands. To install, please check out the installation guide of Git flow at: `https://github.com/nvie/gitflow/wiki/Installation`.

Before we can use Git flow to create and merge branches, we'll need to make an initialization:

```
$ git flow init -d
```

Here `-d` stands for using default branch naming conventions. If you would like to customize, you may omit the `-d` option and answer the questions about `git flow init` command.

This will create `master` and `develop` branches (if not present) and save Git flow-related configuration to the local repository.

Main branches

The branching model defines two main branches: `master` and `develop`. Those two branches exist in the lifetime of the current repository: .

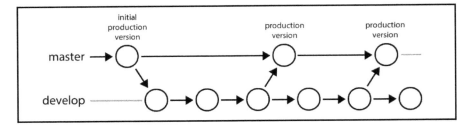

The graph in the preceding shows a simplified relationship between `develop` and `master` branches.

- **Branch master**: The *HEAD* of `master` branch should always contain production-ready source code. It means that no daily development is done on `master` branch in this branching model, and only commits that are fully tested and can be performed with a fast-forward should be merged into this branch.
- **Branch develop**: The *HEAD* of `develop` branch should contain delivered development source code. Changes to `develop` branch will finally be merged into `master`, but usually not directly. We'll come to that later when we talk about `release` branches.

Supporting branches

There are three types of supporting branches in the branching model of Git flow: `feature`, `hotfix`, and `release`. What they roughly do has already been suggested by their names, and we'll have more details to follow.

Feature branches

A feature branch has only direct interactions with the `develop` branch, which means it checks out from a `develop` branch and merges back to a `develop` branch. The feature branches might be the simplest type of branches out of the three.

To create a feature branch with Git flow, simply execute the following command:

```
$ git flow feature start <feature-name>
```

Now Git flow will automatically checkout a new branch named after `feature/<feature-name>`, and you are ready to start development and commit changes occasionally.

After completing feature development, Git flow can automatically merge things back to the `develop` branch by the following command:

```
$ git flow feature finish <feature-name>
```

A feature branch is usually started by the developer who is assigned to the development of that very feature and is merged by the developer him or herself, or the owners of the `develop` branch (for example, if code review is required).

Release branches

In a single iteration of a product, after finishing the development of features, we usually need a stage for fully testing everything, fixing bugs, and actually getting it ready to be released. And work for this stage will be done on release branches.

Unlike feature branches, a repository usually has only one active release branch at a time, and it is usually created by the owner of the repository. When the development branch is reaching a state of release and a thorough test is about to begin, we can then create a release branch using the following command:

```
$ git flow release start <version>
```

From now on, bug fixes that are going to be released in this iteration should be merged or committed to branch `release/<version>` and changes to the current `release` branch can be merged back to the `develop` branch anytime.

If the test goes well and important bugs have been fixed, we can then finish this release and put it online:

```
$ git flow release finish <version>
```

After executing this command, Git flow will merge the current release branch to both `master` and `develop` branches. So in a standard Git flow branching model, the `develop` branch will not be merged into the `master` directly, though after finishing a release, the content on `develop` and `master` branches could be identical (if no more changes are made to the `develop` branch during the releasing stage).

 Finishing the current release usually means the end of the iteration, and the decision should be made with serious consideration.

Hotfix branches

Unfortunately, there's a phenomenon in the world of developers: bugs are always harder to find before the code goes live. After releasing, if serious bugs were found, we would have to use hotfixes to make things right.

A `hotfix` branch works kind of like a release branch but lasts shorter (because you would probably want it merged as soon as possible). Unlike feature branches being checked out from `develop` branch, a `hotfix` branch is checked out from `master`. And after getting things done, it should be merged back to both `master` and `develop` branches, just like a release branch does.

To create a `hotfix` branch, similarly you can execute the following command:

```
$ git flow hotfix start <hotfix-name>
```

And to finish, execute the following command:

```
$ git flow hotfix finish <hotfix-name>
```

Summary of Git flow

The most valuable idea in Git flow beside the branching model itself is, in my opinion, the clear outline of one iteration. You may not need to follow every step mentioned thus far to use Git flow, but just make it fit your work. For example, for small features that can be done in a single commit, you might not actually need a feature branch. But conversely, Git flow might not bring much value if the iteration itself gets chaotic.

Pull request based code review

Code review could be a very important joint of team cooperation. It ensures acceptable quality of the code itself and helps newcomers correct their misunderstanding of the project and accumulate experiences rapidly without taking a wrong path.

If you have tried to contribute code to open-source projects on GitHub, you must be familiar with pull requests or PR. There are actually tools or IDEs with code reviewing workflow built-in. But with GitHub and other self-hosted services like GitLab, we can get it done smoothly without relying on specific tools.

Configuring branch permissions

Restrictions on accessing specific branches like `master` and `develop` are not technically necessary. But without those restrictions, developers can easily skip code reviewing because they are just able to do so. In services provided by the Visual Studio Team Foundation Server, we may add a custom check in policy to force code review. But in lighter services like GitHub and GitLab, it might be harder to have similar functionality.

The easiest way might be to have developers who are more qualified and familiar with the current project have the permissions for writing the `develop` branch, and restrict code reviewing in this group verbally. For other developers working on this project, pull requests are now forced for getting changes they merged.

 GitHub requires an organization account to specify push permissions for branches. Besides this, GitHub provides a status API and can add restrictions to merging so that only branches with a valid status can get merged.

Comments and modifications before merge

A great thing about those popular Git services is that the reviewer and maybe other colleagues of yours may comment on your pull requests or even specific lines of code to raise their concerns or suggestions. And accordingly, you can make modifications to the active pull request and make things a little bit closer to perfect.

Furthermore, references between issues and pull requests are shown in the conversation. This along with the comments and modification records makes the context of current pull requests clear and traceable.

Testing before commits

Ideally, we would expect every commit we make to pass tests and code linting. But because we are human, we can easily forget about running tests before committing changes. And then, if we have already set up continuous integration (we'll come to that shortly) of this project, pushing the changes would make it red. And if your colleague has set up a CI light with an alarm, you would make it flash and sound out.

To avoid breaking the build constantly, you might want to add a pre-commit hook to your local repository.

Git hooks

Git provides varieties of hooks corresponding to specific phases of an operation or an event. After initializing a Git repository, Git will create hook samples under the directory .git/hooks.

Now let's create the file pre-commit under the directory .git/hooks with the following content:

```
#!/bin/sh
npm run test
```

 The hook file does not have to be a bash file, and it can just be any executable. For example, if you want like to work with a Node.js hook, you can update the shebang as #!/usr/bin/env node and then write the hook in JavaScript.

And now Git will run tests before every commit of changes.

Adding pre-commit hook automatically

Adding hooks manually to the local repository could be trivial, but luckily we have npm packages like pre-commit that will add pre-commit hooks automatically when it's installed (as you usually might need to run npm install anyway).

To use the pre-commit package, just install it as a development dependency:

```
$ npm install pre-commit --save-dev
```

It will read your `package.json` and execute npm scripts listed with the field `pre-commit` or `precommit`:

```
{
  ..
  "script": {
    "test": "istanbul cover ..."
  },
  "pre-commit": ["test"]
}
```

 At the time of writing, npm package `pre-commit` uses symbolic links to create Git hook, which requires administrator privileges on Windows. But failing to create a symbolic link won't stop the `npm install` command from completing. So if you are using Windows, you probably might want to ensure `pre-commit` is properly installed.

Continuous integration

The **continuous integration** (**CI**) refers to a practice of integrating multiple parts of a project or solution together regularly. Depending on the size of the project, the integration could be taken for every single change or on a timed schedule.

The main goal of continuous integration is to avoid integration issues, and it also enforces the discipline of frequent automated testing, this helps to find bugs earlier and prevents the degeneration of functionalities.

There are many solutions or services with continuous integration support. For example, self-hosted services like TFS and Jenkins, or cloud-based services like Visual Studio Team Services, Travis-CI, and AppVeyor. We are going to walk through the basic configuration of Travis-CI with our demo project.

Connecting GitHub repository with Travis-CI

We are going to use GitHub as the Git service behind continuous integration. First of all, let's get our GitHub repository and Travis-CI settings ready:

1. Create a correspondent repository as origin and push the local repository to GitHub:

```
$ git remote add origin https://github.com/<username>/<repo>.git
```

```
$ git push -u origin master
```

2. Sign into Travis-CI with your GitHub account at: https://travis-ci.org/auth.
3. Go to the account page, find the project we are working with, and then flick the repository switch on.

Now the only thing we need to make the continuous integration setup work is a proper Travis-CI configuration file. Travis-CI has built-in support for many languages and runtimes. It provides multiple versions of Node.js and makes it extremely easy to test Node.js projects.

Create the file .travis.yml in the root of project with the following content:

```
language: node_js
node_js:
  - "4"
  - "6"
before_script:
  - npm run build
```

This configuration file tells Travis-CI to test with both Node.js v4 and v6, and execute the command npm run build before testing (it will run the npm test command automatically).

Almost ready! Now add and commit the new .travis.yml file and push it to origin. If everything goes well, we should see Travis-CI start the build of this project shortly.

 You might be seeing building status badges everywhere nowadays, and it's easy to add one to the README.md of your own project. In the project page on Travis-CI, you should see a badge next to the project name. Copy its URL and add it to the README.md as an image:

```
![building status](https://api.travis-ci.org/<username>/<repo>.svg)
```

Deployment automation

Rather than a version control tool, Git is also popular for relatively simple deployment automation. And in this section, we'll get our hands on and configure automated deployment based on Git.

Passive deployment based on Git server side hooks

The idea of passive deployment is simple: when a client pushes commits to the bare repository on the server, a `post-receive` hook of Git will be triggered. And thus we can add scripts checking out changes and start deployment.

The elements involved in the Git deployment solution on both the client and server sides includes:

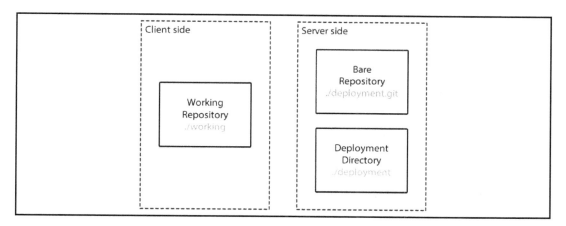

To make this mechanism work, we need to perform the following steps:

1. Create a bare repository on the server with the following command:

```
$ mkdir deployment.git
$ cd deployment.git
$ git init --bare
```

 A bare repository usually has the extension `.git` and can be treated as a centralized place for sharing purposes. Unlike normal repositories, a bare repository does not have the working copy of source files, and its structure is quite similar to what's inside a `.git` directory of a normal repository.

2. Add `deployment.git` as a remote repository of our project, and try to push the `master` branch to the `deployment.git` repository:

```
$ cd ../demo-project
$ git remote add deployment ../deployment.git
$ git push -u deployment master
```

We are adding a local bare repository as the remote repository in this example. Extra steps might be required to create real remote repositories.

3. Add a `post-receive` hook for the `deployment.git` repository. We've already worked with the client side Git hook `pre-commit`, and the server side hooks work the same way.

But when it comes to a serious production deployment, how to write the hook could be a hard question to answer. For example, how do we minimize the impact of deploying new builds?

If we have set up our application with high availability load balancing, it might not be a big issue to have one of them offline for minutes. But certainly not all of them in this case. So here are some basic requirements of the deploy scripts on both the client and server sides:

- The deployment should be proceeded in a certain sequence
- The deployment should stop running services gently

And we can do better by:

- Building outside of the previous deployment directory
- Only trying to stop running services after the newly deployed application is ready to start immediately

Proactive deployment based on timers or notifications

Instead of using Git hooks, we can have other tools pull and build the application automatically as well. In this way, we no longer need the client to push changes to servers separately. And instead, the program on the server will pull changes from a remote repository and complete deployment.

A notification mechanism is preferred to avoid frequent fetching though, and there are already tools like PM2 that have automated deployment built-in. You can also consider building up your own using hooks provided by cloud-based or self-hosted Git services.

Summary

In this final chapter, we built the outline of a complete workflow starting with building and testing to continuous integration and automated deployment. We've covered some popular services or tools and provide other options for readers to discover and explore.

Among the varieties of choice, you might agree that the most appropriate workflow for your team is the workflow that fits the best. Taking people rather than technologies alone into consideration is an important part of software engineering, and it is also the key to keeping the team efficient (and happy, perhaps).

The sad thing about a team, or a crowd of people is that usually only a few of them can keep the passion burning. We've talked about finding the balance point, but that is what we still need to practice. And in most of the cases, expecting every one of your team to find the right point is just unreasonable. When it comes to team projects, we'd better have rules that can be validated automatically instead of conventions that are not testable.

After reading this book, I hope the reader gets the outlines of the build steps, workflow, and of course knowledge of common design patterns. But rather than the cold explanations of different terms and patterns, there are more important ideas I wanted to deliver:

- We as humans are dull, and should always keep our work divided as controllable pieces, instead of acting like a genius. And that's also why we need to *design* software to make our lives easier.
- And we are also unreliable, especially at a scale of some mass (like a team).
- As a learner, always try to understand the reason behind a conclusion or mechanism behind a phenomenon.

Index

www.ingramcontent.com/pod-product-compliance
Lightning Source LLC
Chambersburg PA
CBHW060539060326
40690CB00017B/3541